LONG CIRCUI
IN T.
STAFFORDSHIRE
MOORLANDS

by
JOHN N. MERRILL
(Footslogger)

Maps and photographs by John N. Merrill.

a J.N.M. PUBLICATION

1992

CIRCULAR WALKS by JOHN N. MERRILL

a J.N.M. PUBLICATION,

J.N.M. PUBLICATIONS,
WINSTER,
MATLOCK,
DERBYSHIRE.
DE4 2DQ
☎ **Winster (0629) 650454**
FAX Winster (0629) 650416

Edited, typeset, designed, paged, marketed and distributed by John N. Merrill.

© Text and routes - John N. Merrill 1991.

© Maps and photographs - John N. Merrill 1991.

First Published - December 1991

ISBN 0 907496 98 9

Meticulous research has been undertaken to ensure that this publication is highly accurate at the time of going to press. The publishers, however, cannot be held responsible for alterations, errors or omissions, but they would welcome notification of such for future editions.

Typeset in - Eagle book and bold and Bookman - bold, italic and plain 10pt and 18pt.

Printed by - John N. Merrill at Milne House, Speedwell Mill, Miller's Green, Wirksworth, Derbyshire. DE4 4BL

Cover sketch by John Creber - "Tittesworth Reservoir and Hen Cloud" - © J.N.M. PUBLICATIONS 1991.

An all British product.

CONTENTS

Hi!
- a few notes about
Footslogger.

He was born in the flatlands around Luton in Bedfordshire, but his athletic capabilities soon showed themselves on Sports Day and in the football and cricket teams. Although expelled twice from different schools, he moved to Sheffield and was taken out into the Peak District at the age of 6 1/2. Here he ran up and down the rocks and the sense of enjoyment and freedom has never left him. He was hooked on the outdoors for life. By the age of 15 he had 350 books on the Himalayas and other mountain areas and although failed all eight O levels, he was writing a book on the history of mountaineering! At 16 he soloed the 90 foot high school building and the headmaster rushed him off to Outward Bound Mountain School to be properly trained - he thought it was a fantastic holiday!

At 17 he was chosen with eleven others to go on an expedition to Norway, for a month. Since then he has walked more than 150,000 miles in different parts of the world. He has walked The Cleveland Way 8 times; The Peakland Way 14 times; The Limey Way 14 times; The Pennine Way 4 times; Offa's Dyke 3 times; Pembrokeshire Coast Path 3 times; and all the other official paths at least twice.

He is an avid walker and never known to be really tired; likes to carry heavy loads at 18,000 feet and hates having his socks or shirts washed after a six month walk! His ideal day is a 25 mile walk with three bars of chocolate in his pocket. Having worn out nearly fifty pairs of boots he truly lives upto his nickname, Footslogger!

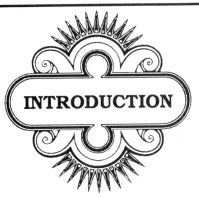

INTRODUCTION

The Staffordshire Moorlands area has long been a favourite walking area of mine, especially around the Manifold Valley and the The Roaches. Some of my early rock climbing was on The Roaches, while in winter I would explore the area on foot looking for the wallabies and visiting Lud Church. The Dane valley is another "special" of mine and I never tire of walking that area.

Whilst the Peak National Park area on the eastern side was familiar to me the western side was new and full of surprises. The Caldon Canal is a jewel and another book of mine explores that fully. The nearby Tittesworth Reservoir and Rudyard Lake came as a surprise, especially the lake lying in such a majestic setting. In the end I did two walks in this area! The Biddulph area came as a shock for I hadn't expected to see such good country here and Knypersley Reservoir is outstanding and one of the finest "long" walks I have made. South-wards is Consall and Caverswall, again excellent walking area with delightful villages but some of the rights of way are little used, but I hope this book encourages to explore here for it is well worth it.

For a long while I couldn't find a really good walk in the Weaver Hills but almost as an afterthought I did! The route from Waterhouses proved exceptional and the return through the dale a sheer delight. Three walks are around the Manifold and Dovedale area, although popular country the routes take you into familiar areas from new angles. The walking for the book began at Onecote on New Years day. It started fine but eight miles out it turned dark and sheeted down with rain. I was soon soaked to the skin and the final three miles in the dark. But for me, an immensely satisfying walk through rolling countryside and a great way to let the new year in! I hope you derive as much pleasure as I have walking these routes and may I wish you

HAPPY WALKING!

John N. Merrill

5

ABOUT THE WALKS

Whilst every care is taken detailing and describing the walk in this book, it should be borne in mind that the countryside changes by the seasons and the work of man. I have described the walk to the best of my ability, detailing what I have found on the walk in the way of stiles and signs. Obviously with the passage of time stiles become broken or replaced by a ladder stile or even a small gate. Signs too have a habit of being broken or pushed over. All the route follow rights of way and only on rare occasions will you have to overcome obstacles in its path, such as a barbed wire fence or electric fence. On rare occasions rights of way are rerouted and these ammendments are included in the next edition.

The seasons bring occasional problems whilst out walking which should also be borne in mind. In the height of summer paths become overgrown and you will have to fight your way through in a few places. In low lying areas the fields are often full of crops, and although the pathline goes straight across it may be more practical to walk round the field edge to get to the next stile or gate. In summer the ground is generally dry but in autumn and winter, especially because of our climate, the surface can be decidedly wet and slippery; sometimes even gluttonous mud!

These comments are part of countryside walking which help to make your walk more interesting or briefly frustrating. Standing in a farmyard up to your ankles in mud might not be funny at the time but upon reflection was one of the highlights of the walk!

The mileage for each walk is based on three calculations -

1. pedometer reading.
2. the route map measured on the map.
3. the time I took for the walk.

I believe the figure stated for each walk to be very accurate but we all walk differently and not always in a straight line! The time allowed for each walk is on the generous side and does not include pub stops etc. The figure is based on the fact that on average a person walks 2 1/2 miles an hours but less in hilly terrain.

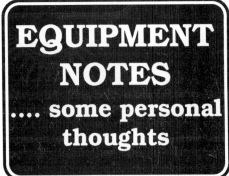

EQUIPMENT NOTES .... some personal thoughts

BOOTS - *preferably with a full leather upper, of medium weight, with a vibram sole. I always add a foam cushioned insole to help cushion the base of my feet.*

SOCKS - *I generally wear two thick pairs as this helps minimise blisters. The inner pair are of loop stitch variety and approximately 80% wool. The outer are a thick rib pair of approximately 80% wool.*

WATERPROOFS - *for general walking I wear a T shirt or cotton shirt with a cotton wind jacket on top. You generate heat as you walk and I prefer to layer my clothes to avoid getting too hot. Depending on the season will dictate how many layers you wear. In soft rain I just use my wind jacket for I know it quickly dries out. In heavy or consistant rain I slip on a neoprene lined gagoule, and although hot and clammy it does keep me reasonably dry. Only in extreme conditions will I don overtrousers, much preferring to get wet and feel comfortable. I never wear gaiters!*

FOOD - *as I walk I carry bars of chocolate, for they provide instant energy and are light to carry. In winter a flask of hot coffee is welcome. I never carry water and find no hardship from not doing so, but this is a personal matter! From experience I find the more I drink the more I want and sweat. You should always carry some extra food such as Kendal Mint Cake, for emergencies.*

RUCKSACKS - *for day walking I use a climbing rucksack of about 40 litre capacity and although it leaves excess space it does mean that the sac is well padded, with an internal frame and padded shoulder straps. Inside apart from the basics for one day I carry gloves, balaclava, spare pullover and a pair of socks.*

MAP & COMPASS - *when I am walking I always have the relevant map - preferably 1:25,000 scale - open in my hand. This enables me to constantly check that I am walking the right way. In case of bad weather I carry a compass, which once mastered gives you complete confidence in thick cloud or mist.*

THE RIVER DANE - 13 MILES

THE RIVER DANE
- 13 miles.
- allow 5 hours

- *Flash—Oliver Hill—Oxenstitch—Readyleech Green—Three Shires Head—Cut-thorn—Crag —Wildboarclough—Clough Brook—Allgreave—Allmeadows—Danebridge—Hangingstone Farm—Lud's Church—Gradbach—Spring Head —Flash.*

Car park: No official car park in Flash. Flash Grid Reference: SK 026672.

- O.S. 1:25,000 Outdoor Leisure Map—The White Peak · west sheet.

- New Inn, Flash; Crag Inn, Wildboarclough; Ship Inn, Danebridge.

ABOUT THE WALK - I first wrote about this walk in 1980 and has since become one of all time favourites! The walk begins from Flash in Staffordshire, the highest village in England at 1,518 feet, and takes you in an anti-clockwise direction to some of my favourite places just inside the Staffordshire and Cheshire counties. These include Three Shires Head, Wildboarclough, Danebridge and Lud's Church. The route is along rights-of-way; some are rarely trodden while others are walked often. To make the walk even more enjoyable there are several inns en route!

Flash was renowned for Flash Money for in the 18th century it was a wintering place for hawkers. While waiting for the summer fairs, the hawkers made flash or counterfeit money on a button press. Living very close to the Derbyshire/Staffordshire border the occupants could avoid paying taxes by slipping across the border when the need arose.

WALKING INSTRUCTIONS - From the church in Flash walk up the road on the right-hand side of the New Inn. On reaching the drive to the last house on your right, turn right then left and follow the walled lane. After 20 yards turn right and now begin heading almost due north to Oxenstitch 3/4 mile away. The path line is faint and the first stile in the gritstone wall has gone. The next two walls that you cross both have ladder type stiles. You descend to a walled grass lane which you follow to the summit of Oliver Hill with the gritstone rocks of Wolf Edge on your left. Ignore two walled tracks on your left as you near the hill summit. From the summit, which is really a very shallow saddle, keep heading northwards and cross two fields descending towards the left-hand side of the farm building Oxenstitch. There is a wooden ladder stile part way down but the stile on to the walled lane as you approach Oxenstitch is missing. At the road is a stone stile and footpath sign. This 1/4 mile section from Flash is the hardest route finding section on the whole walk.

Turn left at Oxenstitch and at the road junction 1/4 mile later turn right to the farm building at Readyleech Green. Here turn left and walk along the gated road. Just over the brow of the hill bear left and descend to a narrow single tracked tarmac lane. Turn left along this lane gradually walking westwards. The walking down this lane is excellent as you follow the line of an old packhorse route. Keep the stream on your left-hand side and after 1/4 mile bear left along the valley bottom keeping the stream still on your left. In half a mile you reach Three Shires Head and Panniers Pool, and two packhorse bridges. This very scenic area makes the walk so worthwhile. There used to be three standing stones here, one for each county— Derbyshire, Staffordshire and Cheshire—but nothing remains today. Cross the River Dane and turn left and follow the curving stony track around the base of Cut-thorn Hill. After 1/4 mile of gentle climbing you reach the tarmac lane and the building, Cut-thorn. The stile and footpath are on the immediate right of the building. The path line is defined as it weaves its way across moorland to the A54 road 1/2 mile away. At the road there is a footpath sign stating Three Shires Head and Crag, towards which you are heading.

Cross the road, climb the stile and begin following the path on the immediate right of a building. Gradually descend, keeping the stone wall on your right, to a gate and track through a small wood to the road just above Crag Hall. descend down the road towards the village of Wildboar clough. Crag Hall is on your right and is owned by Lord Derby. A little further down the road you pass the church dedicated to St. Saviour and shortly afterwards the impressive administrative buildings of the silk mills that once flourished here. The building was until recently the local post office. In the 18th century there were three mills in Wildboarclough and as you descended to the village you would notice the large mill pond on your right in the trees. At the road junction turn left and walk along the road signposted for Wincle.

Two hundred yards from the junction you pass the Crag Inn on your right which does bar snacks and is a free house. A 1/4 mile later on your left is the entrance to Brook Side Cafe and the local post office. Just through the gateway turn right, as footpath signposted and walk beside Clough Brook for 1/4 mile. The path turns into a grassy walled track as it passes a small farm on your right and curves to your left around the edge of a small wood. A 1/4 mile later the track meets another track beside a footpath sign. Turn left up the walled track to the A54 road at Allgreave. Turn right at the road and walk past the Rose and Crown Inn and descend the switchback road and cross the bridge over the brook. At the cross roads just beyond, turn left following the road to Wincle. After 1/4 mile turn left at Allmeadows Farm and follow the footpath sign posted for Danebridge. The sign gives the mileage as 1 mile; it is in fact 1 1/2 miles as the footpath sign at Danebridge states! Walk through the farm and follow the walled lane. As you approach the brook bear right up a gently ascending grass track. The path line is faint but basically you maintain your present height as you contour round the fields above the river and walk on the immediate right of a small wood. Three hundred yards later you reach a farm road via a stile on the left of a gate. Keep straight ahead down the farm road to Bottomley Farm. Leave the farmyard via the stile on the left-hand side and cross the field to Hog Clough. Entering the wooded clough there is a stile and curving path. Cross the brook and ascend to another stile. One final field brings you to Danebridge whose road is reached via stone steps. Turn left into the village passing the Ship Inn.

Continue down the road from the inn and cross the River Dane. As you ascend from the bridge take the second footpath signposted for Back Forest 1 1/2 miles and Gradbach 2 1/2 miles. The path ascends between the houses before entering the wood. To guide you through the wood are yellow marker posts. Part way through the pine wood turn right along a well defined path and ascend to the stile on the wood's edge. From the wood aim for Hangingstone Farm. Walk past the left-hand side of the farm and ascend to the track just beyond. Turn right and follow the track for 1/2 mile. As you do so you have splendid views of The Roaches and Hen Cloud. After 1/2 mile at a gate ascend the stile on the right and turn left following the track on to the moor. The next 1/2 mile is delightful walking along a well defined track. As you walk grouse take to the air startled by your intrusion. Upon reaching a cluster of rocks the track divides. Your route is the left fork but if you have time before taking it, bear right and follow the other track a short distance to see Lud's Church. It is a deep gritstone gorge, 50 feet deep and about 200 feet long and is probably a landslip. Among several stories related to the gorge is one concerning Friar Tuck who held services there. It is also reputed that Robin Hood sometimes hid here when pursued by the sheriff.

From the stones begin descending gradually through Forest Wood. After a little over 1/4 miles the track turns right. Bear left past a footpath signpost and cross the Black Brook via a footbridge. Ascend the track beyond a short distance before turning left through a stile and walking near the river to Gradbach Mill. Follow the mill road to the road from Gradbach. Turn left and shortly afterwards instead of walking down the road you can use a footpath on your left through the fields. A 1/4 mile later where the road and river come together, turn left and cross another footbridge and field to the road on the left of Manor Farm. Turn right and opposite Manor Farm on the summit of the road, ascend the stile on the left-hand side of the gate. The next 1/4 mile of footpath is one not trodden frequently. Once over the stile the next stile is straight ahead on the left of the water trough. Over that one you now walk beside the wall on your left. Stiles and gate openings take you up the fields. At the end of the fifth field you cross a further wall and field to a grass track in front of a walled field. Turn right and follow this descending grass track. It can be readily traced; a 1/4 mile later cross the small brook via a wooden footbridge and the stile is on the left before ascending to the Flash road at Spring Head. Turn left at the road and 3/4 mile later, after ascending most of the way, you pass the house you walked past at the beginning of the walk and descend into Flash.

LONGNOR & WARSLOW
- 12 MILES

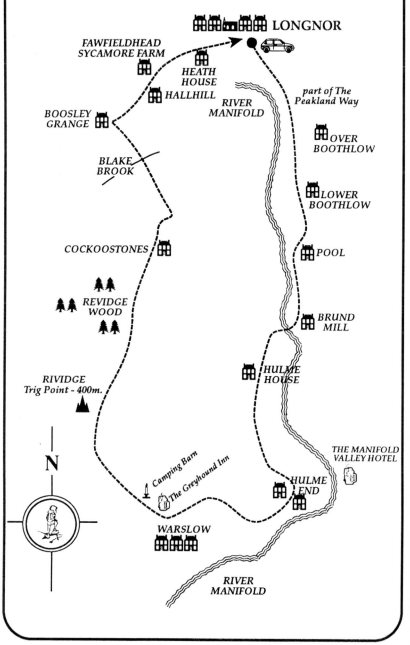

LONGNOR

FAWFIELDHEAD
SYCAMORE FARM

HEATH
HOUSE

HALLHILL

RIVER
MANIFOLD

part of The
Peakland Way

BOOSLEY
GRANGE

OVER
BOOTHLOW

BLAKE
BROOK

LOWER
BOOTHLOW

COCKOOSTONES

POOL

REVIDGE
WOOD

BRUND
MILL

RIVIDGE
Trig Point - 400m.

HULME
HOUSE

N

THE MANIFOLD
VALLEY HOTEL

Camping Barn

The Greyhound Inn

HULME
END

WARSLOW

RIVER
MANIFOLD

LONGNOR & WARSLOW
- 12 MILES
- allow 4 1/2 hours

- Longnor - The Peakland Way - River Manifold - Lower Boothlow - Pool - Brund Mill - Hulme End - Manifold Valley Track - Warslow - Revidge - Trig Point 400 metres - Cuckoostones - Blake Brook - Boosley Grange - Hallhill - Sycamore Farm, Fawfieldhead - Heath House - Longnor.

- O.S. 1:25,000 Outdoor Leisure Series - The-White Peak (West Sheet.)

- Longnor Market Place.

- Hulme End - at start of Manifold Valley Track.

- Several in Longnor, including the Crewe & Harpur Arms, The Grapes and The Cheshire Cheese. In Warslow - The Greyhound Inn.

ABOUT THE WALK - First you descend to Hulme End following my Peakland Way walk. The path crosses fields and comes close to the River Manifold several times. From Hulme End you follow a short section of the Manifold Valley Track before ascending to Warslow with stunning views of the valley. Warslow has an inn. Camping Barn and stocks. You continue ascending, gradually, to near Trig Point 400 with extensive views over much of the western area of the Peak District. You cross fields and brooks back to Longnor. The walk is done clockwise.

WALKING INSTRUCTIONS - Turn left out of the Market Place in Longnor, along the Crowdecote Road. Pass the Cheshire Cheese Inn on your left and a short distance later, turn right, as footpath signed, and descend the farm drive to Folds End. Turn left in the yard to a stile. Ascend this and bear right to another and descend the next field to the bottom lefthand corner to another stile. Through this turn left with the River Manifold on your right. The path is well defined and well stiled. After the fifth stile you move away from the river, cross a farm track, and bear slightly left to a stile. In the subsequent field you bear left slightly to another stile. After this keep the fence on your left and pass Lower Boothlow on your left. You descend a little to a footbridge and stile close to a barn. For the next 1/4 mile you basically keep ahead on the well stiled path to another farm track. Cross this and soon pass a footpath sign to "Brund". A few yards later cross a solitary stone bridge and ascend to your right to the right of Pool Farm. Keep the field boundary on your right and at the fourth stile you are once more near the river. You immediately leave it - it swings away to your right - for another stile. Continue on the path to another stile in the wall before ascending a walled track with the river below you on your right. Keep straight ahead and soon have the field boundary on your left and reach two stiles before gaining the road beside Mill House, Brund - teas available here. Turn right down the road past the mill and over the bridge.

30 yards later turn left through the stile on your left and walk diagonally across the field, aiming for the far righthand corner and another stile. Gain the road and turn left and pass Hulme House almost immediately on your left. Keep on the road for almost 1/2 mile. Where it turns right and ascends, on your left is a stone stile. Pass through this then a wooden one and a few yards later another one. After this keep the hedge on your right to another stile. For the next 1/2 mile basically keep straight ahead to reach the stiles; after the second stile the fence/hedge is on your left. Pass well to the right of Hayesgate Farm and after the stile well beyond it turn right to a stile and road. Turn left to Hulme End 1/4 mile away. At the road junction beside a chapel erected in 1834, turn right to Hulme End Car Park. To your left is the village shop. Through the car park join the Manifold Valley Track. Follow this for a 1/3 mile to the start of a righthand bend. Here you turn right to a kissing gate and footpath sign. Upto this point you have been following my Peakland Way route - 96 miles around the Peak District. Go through the kissing gate and begin ascending with a limestone wall on your right. After a few yards the way becomes clearer with magnificent views of the Ecton area of the Manifold Valley. You basically ascend for the next 1/2 mile, passing through a stile on the way. Don't ascend the wall but follow it round to your right and descend slightly to road from Ecton. Turn right and a short distance later turn left and left again into Warslow village.

Turn right onto the Leek road - just ahead are the stocks. Ascend the road passing the Greyhound Inn on your right and soon afterwards the Warslow Moors Camping Barn. 30 yards later where the road bears right keep straight ahead on footpath signed track. 1/4 mile along the track and before it turns left and descends go through the stile on your right. Keeping the same height as the track, cross two fields to a stile - the walls are now gritstone. Over the stile turn right onto a defined path and ascend to the Leek road. Turn left then right at a stile and follow a defined track. After the next stile the track bears left and passes an oak wood on your right. After this is a stile and simply follow the track to pine trees close to the trig point 400 metres. The views here are panoramic. Continue on the track and slowly descend. After 1/2 mile join another and keep straight ahead and soon pass Cuckoostones on your left. Just afterwards gain the Longnor Road - B5053.

Turn right and 40 yards later turn left onto a track. Almost immediately it forks and take the righthand branch and descend. Pass through a gate and soon afterwards go through a stone stile on your right towards a barn. Just before it turn left through a stile and descend the field aiming for another stile to the left of another barn. After this keep the field boundary - fence - on your left to a stile and footbridge over Blake Brook. Over the bridge keep the gritstone wall on your left to a stile. The next one is just ahead by the gate. Keep ahead in the next field aiming for the far lefthand corner where there are stiles and bridge over the stream. Ascend to the right of Boosley Grange via two stiles. Just past the Grange turn left onto a track and before the wall turn right and descend steeply to footbridge. Over this keep the hawthorn boundary on your left to a stile then solitary gatepost as you ascend to a stile by an electric pylon. Continue ascending to Hallhill and stile. Pass through the farm to the left of the house to a path sign. Turn right to a stile. The next is by a gate and after this you descend to a stile and footbridge. Over this and as indicated by the signs walk around the righthand side of Sycamore Farm and gain the road at Fawfieldhead.

Turn right then left and in 100 yards turn right at the stile by the gate. Go diagonally across the field to a stile and footpath sign and descend to the right of a small cleft. At the bottom is a stile and path sign. Bear left and ascend to Heath House and the Longnor Road. Turn right and follow the road back to Longnor and its Market Place.

LONGNOR - The area around the church and Market Place is well worth exploring. The toll board in the Market Place records the tolls charged in 1903 - "every basket of eggs or other articles for sale...One Penny". The classical church was built in 1780. The outside looks like two storeys but inside is a false ceiling. There are many gravestones of note including one to a former blacksmith and one to William Billings, who died on January 25th 1791, aged 112.

THE PEAKLAND WAY - A 96 mile circular walk around the Peak District, devised and created by John Merrill. A delightful week's walk seeing the scenic splendour of the Peak District in one fell swoop!

THE ROACHES - 16 MILES

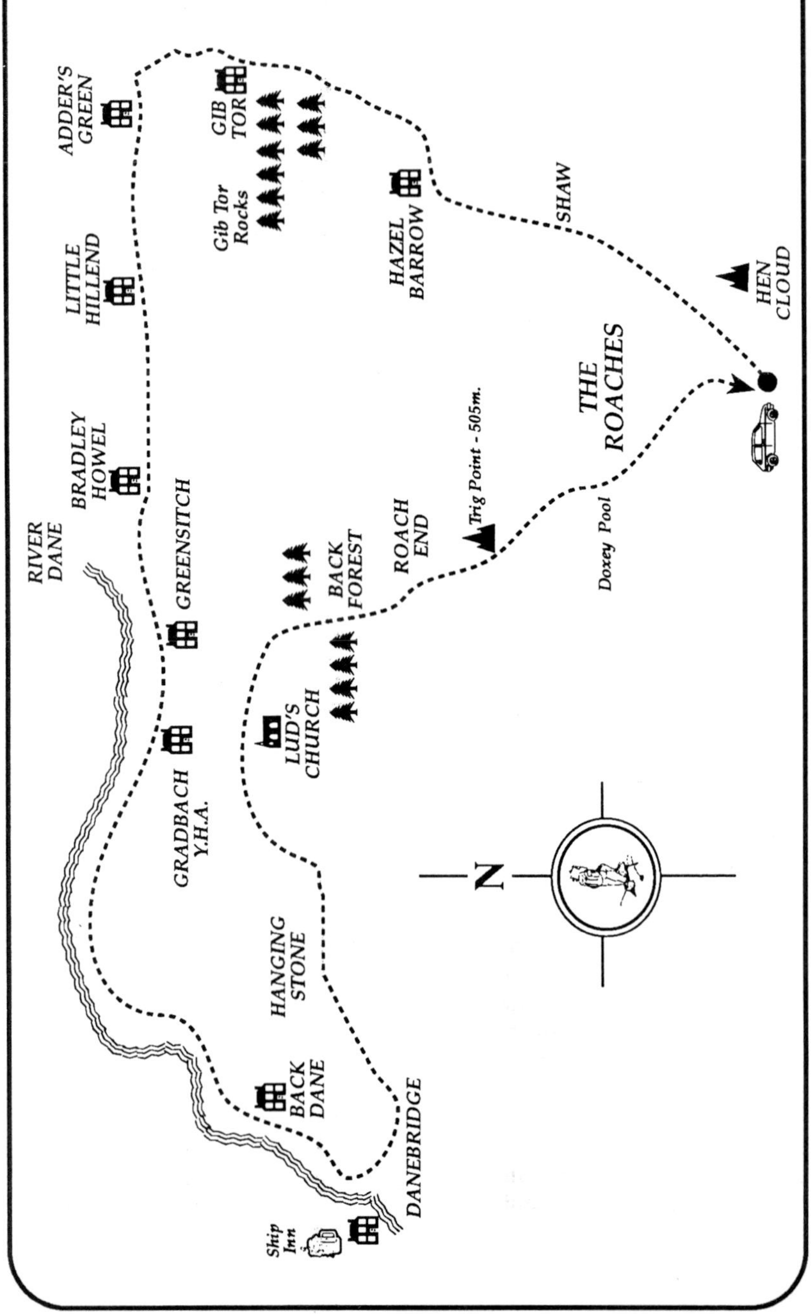

ADDER'S GREEN

GIB TOR

Gib Tor Rocks

LITTLE HILLEND

HAZEL BARROW

SHAW

HEN CLOUD

BRADLEY HOWEL

GREENSITCH

RIVER DANE

THE ROACHES

Trig Point - 505m.

ROACH END

Doxey Pool

BACK FOREST

LUD'S CHURCH

GRADBACH Y.H.A.

N

HANGING STONE

BACK DANE

Ship Inn

DANEBRIDGE

18

THE ROACHES
- 16 MILES
- allow 5 to 6 hours

- Roaches Car Park - Shaw - Hazel Barrow - Gib Torr - Adder's Green - Little Hillend - Bradley Howel - Greensitch - Gradbach YHA - River Dane - Back Dane - Danebridge - Hanging Stone - Lud's Church - Back Forest - Roach End - Trig Point 505 metres - The Roaches - Doxey Pool - Rockhall - Roaches Car Park.

 - 1:25,000 Outdoor Leisure Map - The White Peak - West Sheet.

 - Beneath The Roaches - Grid Ref. SK004622.

- None actually on the walk but at Danebridge, 1/4 mile to the N.W. is The Ship Inn complete with Hiker's bar!

ABOUT THE WALK - The Roaches and surrounding rocky moorland area is one of the finest walking areas in Staffordshire Moorlands. It is wild and remote in winter but in summer is full of heather, abundant woods and red grouse. This circular route takes around the whole area to explore and see the numerous rock shapes - edges and impressive boulders - as well as visiting the River Dane and the awesome Lud's Cave. The climax to the walk is the final two miles as you walk along the spine and underneath the impressive gritstone outcrop - the Roaches - with the impressive Hen Cloud just beyond. I never tire of walking this area and despite countless walks here, I always learn and see something new. As to whether you will see any of the wallabies, one never knows. I have seen them and people have sent me photographs of them, but of late they have eluded me. Twenty years ago I saw over thirty leaping over a wall; a sight I will never forget. On another occasion I came face to face with one in the snow!

WALKING INSTRUCTIONS - From the car park walk down the road a few yards to the gate and track into The Roaches Estate, on your left. You will be walking in and out of the estate much of the walk. Walk up the track and follow it round to your left, passing between The Roaches and Hen Cloud. The former you descend and rejoin this track at the end of the walk. Keep on this weaving track close to the moorland boundary for almost a mile to a gate and Roaches Estate plaque. Here continue ahead on the track for just over 1/4 mile to a cattle-grid and minor road beyond. Turn right along the road and in just over 1/4 mile follow it round to your left with a road junction on your right. In another 200 yards reach a road junction beside Hazel Barrow Farm. Cross over and walk along the track on the immediate right of Corner House. Follow this track past some large boulders to a stile. Continue ahead on the defined path and in 1/4 mile at another rocky outcrop ahead, turn right and descend slightly as you curve round past a water pipe to a stile and entrance into a pine forest. Continue ahead on the wide track through the forest and soon descend to the road opposite the house Gib Torr. As you gained the forest you will have seen Gib Torr Rocks on your left.

Turn left and ascend the road to a T junction. Go straight across and walk along the track towards Ann Roach Farm. At the end of the first field where the track bears left, turn right, as footpath signed, to a stile. Cross this and continue through the field aiming for the lefthand side Adder's Green farm. Upon gaining the wall turn left and follow the field boundary round to two stiles. Cross these and cross the track to Ann Roach Farm. Continue across the middle of a field aiming for the lefthand edge of a circular wall. Walk beside this wall to a stile. You now keep the field boundary on you left then right as you descend gently towards the righthand side of Little Hillend. Cross the road beyond to a gate and follow a track with a wall on your left to a solitary house/farm and walk past this on its righthand side, following a walled track. Continue ahead where you leave the track across a field aiming for a stile well to the right of a solitary barn. Through this turn left and descend to a stile and road. Turn right and in a few yards almost opposite Bradley Howel, turn left over the stile and descend the field to its bottom left to a stile and cross the stream beyond. Diagonally ascend the field aiming for the corner of the second field on your left, where there is a stile. Cross the corner of the field to the field wall and keep this on your left to the next stile in the lefthand corner. Over this descend to a gate and Greenstitch Farm. Walk past the farm on your left on the farm track to the minor Gradbach road. Turn left then right and descend the drive to Gradbach Youth Hostel.

At the Youth Hostel turn left and follow the path to some steps and a stile. Continue along the path close to the field boundary and in 1/4 mile reach the footbridge over Black Brook and back into The Roaches Estate. Ascend a few yards before turning right - footpath signed - Danebridge. For the next two miles you are mostly in forest with the River Dane on your right. The path is well defined and signed and for the first 3/4 mile you keep close to the river and gain a stile. Shortly afterwards you begin leaving the river and gain another stile on the western boundary of The Roaches Estate. You leave the main forest behind as you contour round the valley side on the defined and well stiled path and in another 1/2 mile reach the track of Back Dane. Turn right down it for a few yards before turning left and following a track then path as you enter woodland and the river is nearby on your right. In 3/4 mile you reach another stile and leave the woodland and walk close to the river as you curve round to the bridge over the River Dane at Danebridge.

If you want to go to The Ship Inn, continue to the bridge and turn right and follow the road to the inn, about 1/4 mile away. If you don't want the inn, just before the bridge turn left up the steps with a stream on your left and ascend through pine trees to a footbridge. Cross this and continue to the boundary of the forest. Cross a stile and ascend the field well to the left of Hanging stone Farm. Gain a stile in the wall and turn right passing the farm on your right and follow a track for the next 1/2 mile, passing the prominent Hanging Stone on your left. A permissive path leads upto to this interesting rock formation. In 1/2 mile turn sharp left onto another track and re-enter The Roaches Estate.

The track curves round the hillside to a stile. Keep to the lefthand path, signed Gradbach, and keep a wall on your left and in another 1/2 mile reach a path junction with a rocky outcrop on your left. Take the righthand path - a stone marker points to Lud"s Church. Follow this path and in about 200 yards reach the narrow entrance into Lud's Church on your right. It is well worth walking through this magnificent cleft and you rejoin the path on the other side. If you don't want to explore this historical and geological wonder, then continue on the path. The path continues through Forest Wood and for much of the time keep to the southern fringe of the forest. In 3/4 mile from Lud's Church gain a line of beech trees. Here bear right and leave the forest and ascend close to a wall on your left to the track, gained by a stile, then road at Roach End.

Cross the road and continue ascending on the defined path to the summit of The Roaches, the trig point 505 metres, 1/2 mile away. Continue along the spine of the ridge and in 3/4 mile pass Doxey Pool on your left. Little over 1/4 mile later leave the ridge and descend to the first tier The Roaches. Bear left along the path through the pine trees with the impressive 90 foot high gritstone face on your left - especially The Sloth, an impressive overhanging rock climbing route! Soon after turn right again and descend the steps to the lower tier and pass Rockhall on your left. A short distance later regain your starting out path and turn right back to the road and carpark.

ROUND TITESWORTH RESERVOIR - 8 MILES

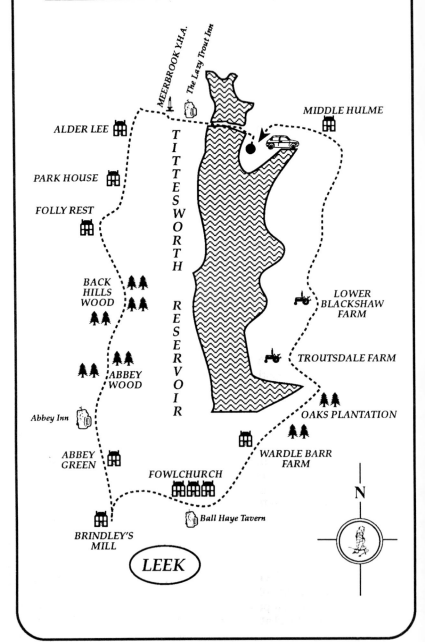

MEERBROOK Y.H.A.

The Lazy Trout Inn

MIDDLE HULME

ALDER LEE

TITTESWORTH RESERVOIR

PARK HOUSE

FOLLY REST

BACK HILLS WOOD

LOWER BLACKSHAW FARM

TROUTSDALE FARM

ABBEY WOOD

Abbey Inn

OAKS PLANTATION

ABBEY GREEN

WARDLE BARR FARM

FOWLCHURCH

Ball Haye Tavern

N

BRINDLEY'S MILL

LEEK

ROUND TITTESWORTH RESERVOIR - 8 MILES
- allow 3 hours.

- *Tittesworth Reservoir Car Park - Meerbrook - Alder Lee - Park House - Folly Rest - Back Hills Wood - Abbey Wood - Abbey Green - Brindley's Mill - Fowlchurch - Ball Haye Green - Wardle Barr Farm - Oaks Plantation - Troutsdale Farm - Lower Blackshaw Farm - Middle Hulme - Tittesworth Reservoir Car Park.*

- *1:25,000 Outdoor Leisure Map - The Peak District - West Sheet.*

- *Tittesworth Reservoir - Grid Ref. SK994604.*

- *The Lazy Trout, Meerbrook; Abbey Inn, Abbey Green; Ball Haye Tavern, Ball Haye Green.*

ABOUT THE WALK - A short one but a walk around a particularly fine area following mostly little used paths. You see the site of an ancient abbey upon which the fame of Leek grew. To get to the vantage point you walk through a magnificent wood - Back Hills Wood. To complete your encirclement of the reservoir you walk around the northern fringe of Leek with the option of visiting Brindley's Mill - the father of the British Canal system -you can also start the walk from Leek. The route along the eastern side of the reservoir is through further woodland and across fields. As with almost all the walk you are always within sight of the reservoir but returning to the start you have impressive views of the Roaches and Hen Cloud that form a magnificent backdrop to the walk. The walk is done in an anti-clockwise direction and makes a very pleasant summer's evening walk with a pub en route!

WALKING INSTRUCTIONS - From the car park return to the minor road and turn left and follow the road across the northern end of the reservoir. Continue on past the Lazy Trout Inn and Meerbrook YHA. keeping straight ahead at the road junction. Less than a 1/4 mile later and before Broad Lea Farm on your right, turn left to a stile in a field corner. Keep the fence on your immediate right and reach a track at Alder Lee Farm (in a ruinous state). Keep straight ahead to a footbridge and stile. Cross the subsequent field ascending slightly to reach another footbridge. Over this keep the field boundary on your right for three fields to a stile with date stone - 1849 - and track from Gunside. Cross the track to a stile to the right of the gate. Bear left and walk down the field and past Park House with monkey puzzle tree in the garden. Cross the subsequent field to your right to a bend in the field, where there is a stile. Cross the next field to the far left hand corner to a stile and road close to Folly Rest Farm.

Turn right along the road past the farm and begin descending the road a few yards and turn left over a stone stile. Descend the field keeping a fence on your left and cross a wide footbridge at the bottom and bear right towards a gate - the stile is behind the holly bush and enter Back Hills Wood. The path ascends to your right and follow its upward rightwards trend to a stile in the top righthand corner of the wood. Cross the field beyond aiming towards a thin plantation of beech trees. Gaining them turn left and walk along the woods edge and gain a track. Follow it round to your right into Abbey Wood. Leave the track to your left to reach a stile on your left on the wood's perimeter. In the field beyond keep the fence on your right at first before descending to a stile and car park of Abbey Inn. As you descend on your left is Abbey Farm. Gain the road beyond the inn and turn left along it and cross a bridge over a wide stream. Continue along the road and take the first road on your left. If you keep straight ahead you reach Brindley's Mill.

Keep on this road past the houses to its end and enter Fowlchurch Gardens. Just after the tennis courts turn left along the drive into the formal gardens. Keep to the righthand path and pass through a gate and across a lawn to Fowlchurch Road. Turn right along it past the entrance to the baths to a road. On your left is Ball Haye Lodge. Turn left along the road through Ball Haye Green, passing Ball Haye Tavern. Soon after pass the Post Office and playground. Just after turn left along Tittesworth Avenue and left again inbetween houses 33 and 35, along a track. Turn right along the first track on your right and walk past the school playing fields and school before descending to Wardle Barn Farm. Walk past the farm on your left to a stile and gain the reservoir road. Descend a few yards to a stile on your right and just after a long footbridge over a stream. Ascend the field beyond keeping the field boundary on your left, with the woodland of Oaks Plantation on your left over the fence.

Ascend the field for 1/4 mile to a stile on your left. Go through this and along the edge of the field to another stile. Turn right to another stile and partway through the next field turn right keeping to the high ground to reach a stile on your left. Descend steeply - often overgrown in summer - and cross a stream via footbridge part of the round the reservoir walk. On the other side of the bridge turn right following a small path that ascend to a stile. Continue ascending to your left to another stile and walk beside the field hedge to another stile and the farm drive from Troutsdale Farm. Turn left along the drive to the farm taking the second track on your right. At the end turn right over the stile and walk around the field to your left to a stile. Continue ahead with a small wood on your right to a stile. Keep the field boundary on your right to another stile and shortly afterwards another with a footbridge on your right.

Cross the field to Lower Blackshaw Farm. Walk around the left of the main building, as guided by stiles and white arrows. Keep the field hedge on your right to a stile on your right. Enter the edge of a small coppice and walk to the otherside where turn left and continue just inside the the trees to a stile and footbridge. Ascend to another stile and keep the wall on your left to a stile and minor road near New Cottage. Turn left along the road passing Middle Hulme and Marsh Farm before reaching the entrance to Tittesworth Reservoir car park, 1/2 mile later.

TITTESWORTH & RUDYARD RESERVOIRS - 14 MILES

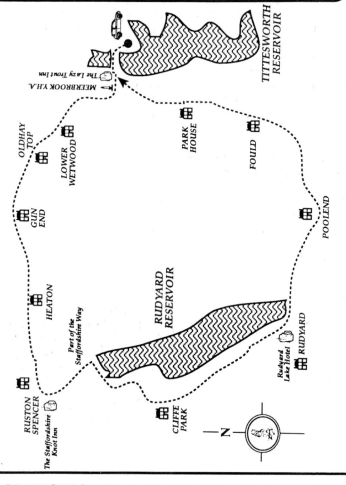

TITTESWORTH RESERVOIR

The Lazy Trout Inn

← MEERBROOK Y.H.A.

OLDHAY TOP

LOWER WETWOOD

PARK HOUSE

FOULD

GUN END

POOLEND

HEATON

RUDYARD RESERVOIR

Part of the Staffordshire Way

RUDYARD

Rudyard Lake Hotel

RUSTON SPENCER

The Staffordshire Knot Inn

CLIFFE PARK

N

THE STAFFORDSHIRE WAY - 90 mile long distance walk from Mow Cop to Kinver Edge. Developed and waymarked by the Staffordshire County Council.

RUDYARD LAKE - Built in 1796 by John Rennie as a canal feeder reservoir. Originally for the nearby Caldon Canal but now used to supply approximately 100 miles of waterways. Like Tittesworth Reservoir you can walk all around the lake - about 5 miles. Their are boat trips, boat hire, railway and other activities. An Information centre is situated near the dam wall.

TITTESWORTH & RUDYARD
RESERVOIRS - 14 MILES
- allow 5 1/2 hours.

- *Tittesworth Reservoir Car Park - Meerbrook - Lower Wetwood - Oldhay Top - Gun End - Heaton - Rushton Spencer - Staffordshire Way - Rudyard Reservoir - Rudyard - Poolend - Fould - Park House - Meerbrook - Tittesworth Reservoir Car Park.*

- *O.S. 1:25,000 Outdoor Leisure Series - The White Peak - West Sheet.*

- *Tittesworth Reservoir - where walk begins.*

- *also at Rushton Spencer and Rudyard.*

- *The Lazy Trout Inn, Meerbrook; Knot Inn, Rushton Spencer; and Rudyard Lake Hotel, Rudyard. Teas/refreshments can be obtained (during the season) at Tittesworth Reservoir, Rudyard Dam and at Gun End Farm.*

ABOUT THE WALK - Starting in the shadow of the magnificent Roaches, your first cross fields and moorland just inside the Peak District National Park to Gun End. All the time are views to the Roaches and Tittesworth Reservoir. You cross further fields and hamlets to Rushton Spencer and the Staffordshire Way. You follow the way southwards above and close to the attractive Rudyard Reservoir. Crossing the dam wall you begin following little used rights of way back to Tittesworth; again the views to the Roaches dominates the scene. For the ornithologist the area is rich in bird life with a wide variety of habitats. Either as an extension to the walk (s) in their own right, you can walk around both Rudyard and Tittesworth Reservoirs - about 5 miles each.

WALKING INSTRUCTIONS - From the car park at Tittesworth Reservoir, walk along the driveway to the road and turn left, crossing the northern end of the reservoir. Walk into Meerbrook village - winner of Best Kept Village competitions - and just past the Lazy Trout Inn on your right, turn right along a minor road - to Roche Grange. After 1/4 mile pass Lea Farm on your right and just after on your left is a gate and footpath sign. Turn left here and ascend gently to your right to a stile. Cross the next field to your right to a track at a field corner. Turn left along the track with the field boundary on your left. After a few yards the track bears right to the righthand corner of the field and a gate. Go through and keep straight ahead on the track with the field hedge on your right. Follow the track round to your right and now a concrete one, as you ascend to Lower Wetwood From. Bear right through the farmyard and follow another concrete track curving to your right and descending a short distance. On the first righthand bend on your left is a wooden stile and footpath sign. Turn left and ascend past solitary trees to a stile and footbridge. In the next field aim for the lefthand side of Oldhay Top Farm. Here in the wall is a stile and path sign. On the otherside reach a concrete track and turn left along it. Keep on this track for just over 1/4 mile to a cattle grid. Just after bear right along the track passing moorland on either side. In another 1/4 mile the track turns sharp left and follow this now tarred track to another lefthand corner. Here turn right over a stile and follow another track with the field wall on your left. After 1/4 mile you descend and in 1/2 mile reach the houses of Gun End.

At the minor road here turn left along it for 1/4 mile to the first lefthand bend. Turn right, as footpath signed - Gighall. In a few yards the track turns left and you follow it past Hawksley Farm to a footbridge by a ford. Keep on the track for over 1/2 mile. Sometimes it is well defined and others a little overgrown. At the end turn left along another track towards the hamlet of Heaton. Before reaching the houses turn right at a wooden stile and keep the field boundary on your left to reach two stone stiles. Just after is another stile a little to your left. Descend the next field to a stone stile and just after is a wooden stile. A few yards later gain a track then minor road. Ignore the turning on your left and at the next junction is the drive to Wormhill Farm. At its start on the left is a stile and path. Through this keep to the upper part of the field as you curve round to stiles and a footbridge before gaining the track past Marsh Side. At the road beyond turn left and cross the A523 road in Rushton Spencer.

Keep straight ahead along the road past the houses to the Knot Inn on your left. On its righthand side gain the Staffordshire Way. Turn left along it through a car park and along the line of an old railway. For the next 3 1/2 miles to the dam wall of Rudyard Reservoir you follow the Staffordshire Way. The signs are intermittent but most of the route is on a well defined track. First you follow the old railway line for nearly a mile to a car park at the northern end of Rudyard Lake. Hear turn right and follow the track around the lake before it ascends and bears left through woodland to the impressive castellated building - Cliffe Park. Keep on the track past it and through the woodland of Rea Cliffe Wood. A mile from Cliffe Park the track bears right and a few yards later you turn left, as Staffordshire Way signed, and soon turn left on a track and descend. Shortly you join a drive which you follow to your right before turning left at a footpath sign and descending to the dam wall; to your right is Rudyard Lake Hotel.

Here at the dam wall you leave the Staffordshire Way and walk across the wall to the Rudyard Lake Railway. Cross the track to a kissing gate and ascend the steps in woodland to a stile at the top. Keep the field boundary on your left to reach the stiles before descending to the right of Greentree Farm. Cross the minor road to a stile and descend the field to a footbridge, another stile and minor road. Go straight across, as footpath signed, and ascend the open field to the hedge on your left. Keep the hedge on your left to a wooden stile. Continue on to another, then a stile and footbridge. Cross this to a stile by a pine wood. Keep this on your left to a stile beneath the road. Beat right keeping the road on your left to a stile by the road junction at Poolend.

Turn left along the A523 road for a few yards before turning right down the farm road to Poolend Farm. Just past the farm on your left turn left through a gate and reach a stile. This right of way is little used as you keep to the field edge for 1/4 mile before ascending a defined track to a gate with Lower Foker Farm on your left. The right of way from here to Fould Villa Farm is blocked. Instead turn right along the track to the minor road. Turn left and at the T junction a little later turn left and in 1/4 mile pass Fould Villa Farm on your left. Keep on this road for the next 3/4 mile to Folly Rest Farm on your right. Just after on your left is the stile, with steps, and footpath sign. Ascend this and bear right to a track and stone stile. Bear left in the next field aiming for the middle of the buildings of Park House. Go through two gates and bear right to a stile and track. Cross this to a stile with a date stone - 1849. Keep the field boundary - mostly a fence - on your left to a footbridge in 1/3 mile. All the time are superb views of The Roaches and Tittesworth Reservoir. Cross the next field to another footbridge. Over this aim for the right of Alder Lee to a stile. Continue ahead to the road on the western edge of Meerbrook. Turn right into the village, Youth Hostel and The Lazy Trout Inn. Retrace your steps back to the car park.

TITTESWORTH RESERVOIR - A 4 1/2 mile (7km) walk can be made around the reservoir - about 3 hours. The reservoir is a good place for ornithology with more than 150 different species recorded. Canada geese, greylag geese, grey heron, coots, moorhens, kingfishers, linnets, skylarks, pied wagtails and pintails can be seen during the year. Ospreys are sighted occasionally and a hide at the northern end gives a perfect location for watching the great crested grebe. A visitors centre is situated at the end of the car park.

BIDDULPH MOOR - 12 MILES

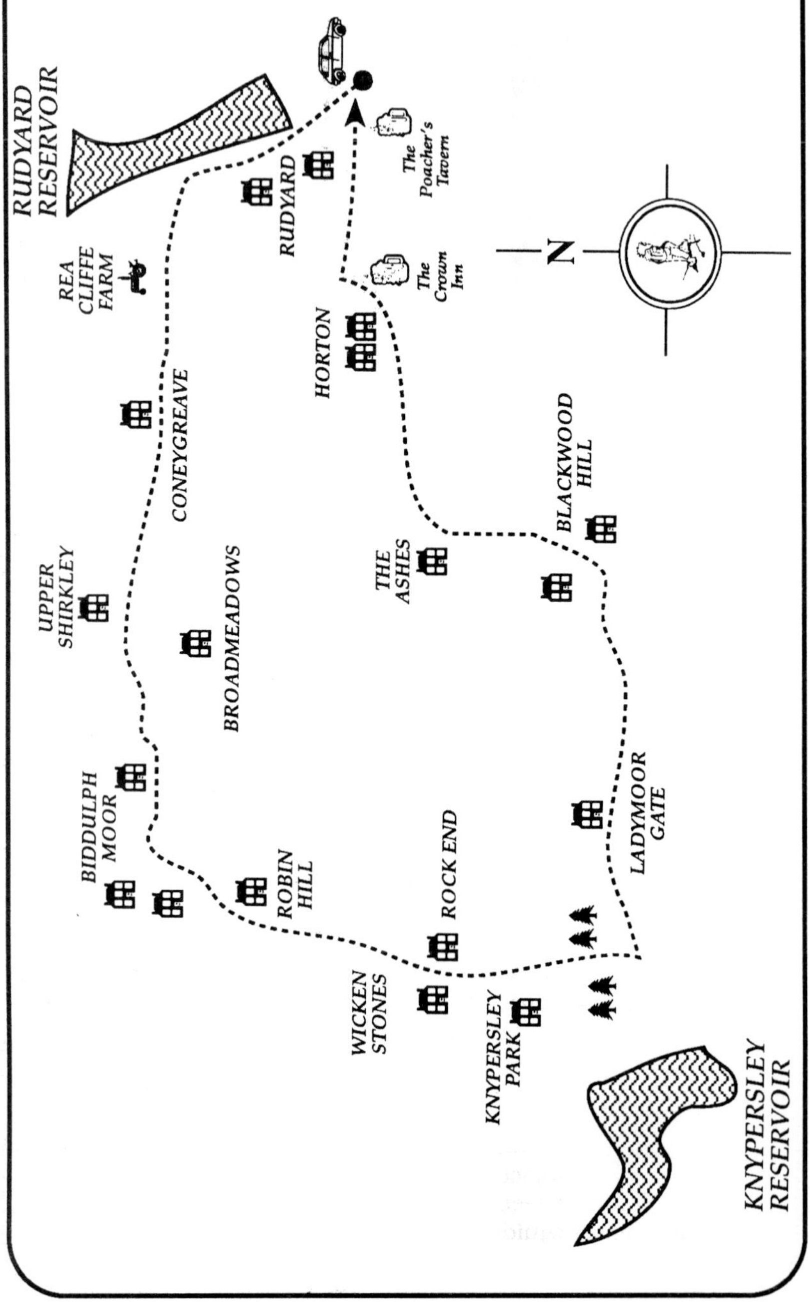

RUDYARD RESERVOIR

The Poacher's Tavern

RUDYARD

REA CLIFFE FARM

The Crown Inn

N

HORTON

CONEYGREAVE

BLACKWOOD HILL

UPPER SHIRKLEY

BROADMEADOWS

THE ASHES

BIDDULPH MOOR

ROBIN HILL

ROCK END

LADYMOOR GATE

WICKEN STONES

KNYPERSLEY PARK

KNYPERSLEY RESERVOIR

BIDDULPH MOOR
- 12 MILES
- allow 4 to 5 hours.

- Rudyard Reservoir Car Park - Lake Railway -Rudyard - Rea Cliffe Farm - Coneygreave - Biddulph Moor - Robin Hill - Wicken Stones - Knypersley Park - Ladymoor Gate - Blackwood Hill - The Ashes - Horton - Rudyard - Car Park.

- O.S. 1:25,000 Pathfinder Series Sheet No.SJ85/95 - Kidsgrove and Leek.

- Beside old railway line - signed "Rudyard Lake Car Park", just east of Rudyard off the B5331 road. Grid Ref. SJ956579.

Rudyard Lake Hotel & the Poachers Tavern at Rudyard; The Foxhound, Biddulph Moor and The Crown Inn, Horton.

ABOUT THE WALK - A walk through a mostly unspoilt area of rolling hills and rocky outcrops. The views are extensive, especially to Mow Cop. The walk combines a mixture of lofty heights, field walking, woodland and attractive old buildings. The rock outcrops of the Biddulph Moor area provide fascinating exploring and in the Horton area you come to some exceptionally beautiful places. The walk is a good introduction to the area and can be linked with other walks in this book that explore adjacent areas to this walk, notably Knypersley Reservoir. As can be seen from the inns listed above, there are three inns placed almost equidistantly apart!

31

WALKING INSTRUCTIONS - From the car park walk northwards along the line of the old railway, with the track of the "Lake Railway" on your right. In just over 1/4 mile reach, "The Dam Station (Halt)", and turn left over the footbridge and walk along the dam wall. Keep straight ahead at the end and ascend the path to the right of the drive to Rudyard Lake Hotel. At the end of the path turn right along the road for a few yards to Glenora House on your left. Here turn left onto the signposted path - "Horton Lodge 1/4 miles & Cliffe Park Station 2 1/4 miles." The track in less than 1/4 mile curves right around a caravan site on your right, before bearing left then right - following Staffordshire Way signs to a track close to the lake; approximately 1/2 mile from road. Here turn left and walk up the track - "Reacliffe Road" - to the minor road at the top, with Rea Cliffe Farm on your right. Keep to the righthand road and descend and in a 1/3 mile reach a T junction. Continue ahead for another 100 yards to where the road turn right with Coneygreave house on your left.

Here leave the road and follow the path on the immediate right of the house, via a stile and footpath sign. You keep the field boundary on your left and at the end of the first field cross a stile and footbridge to gain a track. Continue ahead on this track and where it divides for Taylor's Barn Farm, on your left, take the right branch and continue on the track for more than 1/4 mile. Where it bears right to to Shirkley Hall, go over the stile beside the track and ascend the field towards its top lefthand corner where there is a stile. Continue ahead with the field wall on your left to another stile. Continue ahead with the field boundary on your left to another stile and road on the edge of Biddulph Moor. Extensive views from this area.

Turn half left and walk along "Hot Lane" and just past the Foxhound Inn turn right through the stile and keep the field hedge on your left to a stile and continue on to the next and gain a minor road. Turn left and keep right at the next junction and 100 yards later at the next T junction, turn right. A few yards later opposite "Springfields Farm", turn left along the track and pass the gardens of two houses on your right before entering the grounds of a house; here turn right at the stile and descend the field to the road - "Under the Hill." Turn left along the road and at the road junction left again. In a few yards the road turns sharp left, here turn right on the track and walk past "Vern Lea" house on your left and at the end of the garden turn left along another track. Reach two stiles before heading for the righthand side of the main building of Biddulph Moor Mill, where there is a stile. Walk through the works - "Autopress" - to the main road.

Turn right and in about 100 yards opposite "Maccstone" in Robin Hill, turn right to a stile and descend to another. Here bear left with the field boundary on your left to a gate and stile. Cross the next field to the righthandside of the farm; ahead can be seen the impressive Wicken Stones which you walk to the right of. Descend the next field to the lefthand corner and stile. Bear left keeping the field edge on your right and Wickenstone Farm. Gaining the farm track go straight across through a gate and cross the field to a gate in its lefthand corner. Continue with the wall on your left and the western side of the stones on your left. At the end of the field gain a stile and follow the field boundary around to your left to another stile by a path sign and gain the road at Rock End. Turn right then left and walk along "Lodge Barn Lane". In 1/4 mile reach the buildings of Knypersley Park on your right. Here the lane turns left. Keep ahead for a couple of yards before turning left on the path, with the wall on your left. The path keeps to the edge of the woodland and in 1/4 mile at your second stile, turn left and follow the path down through the woodland to a footbridge. Continue on the path ascending gently to the righthand side of a farm, where there is a stiled fenced path. Continue past the farm to the road.

Turn left up the lane to the road junction at Ladymoor Gate, 1/3 mile away. Here turn right and in a few yards left, at the stile and footpath sign. Keep the field boundary on your left to the next stile, then cross the next to the stile in the far righthand corner. Continue with the hedge on your left to another stile. Just past this one turn left over another one and keep a ditch on your right as you descend the field to a stile with woodland on your left. Here gain a track and follow this as it ascends close to the field boundary on your left. In 1/4 mile you pass a house on your left and just after leave the track and turn left through the stile and ascend the field to the top righthand corner to a stile, pathsign and road at Blackwood Hill. Turn right and in a few yards just past the entrance to a farm on your right, turn left at the stile and path sign. Cross the field passing Grange Farm on your right. Past the farm buildings keep near the righthand edge of the field to a pass a well before reaching a stile and drive at Small Lane. Go straight across the courtyard to a large white metal gate.

Descend the field diagonally left to reach a stone footbridge and stile beyond. Ascend the next field to a stile and two more fields to a stile before "The Ashes" house. Gaining the track here - a bridleway - turn right and follow this grass track for 1/2 mile to the minor road at Damslane. Go straight across to another track and in 1/4 mile gain another lane. Follow this for a few yards and where it turns left, go through a small gate and follow the well defined path close to the field edge on your right. Pass through several small gates before gaining the footbridge over Horton Brook. Horton church acts as a good guideline as you aim for the righthand side of it. Cross the footbridge and ascend keeping the fence on your right before gaining two stiles and land from Horton. Go straight across to another stile and cross the field to another stile with the Crown Inn on your immediate left.

Turn left past the inn and Horton Church, dedicated to St Michael, to the road junction. Straight ahead is the "Old Vicarage" dated 1753. Turn right and descend the lane to where it turns sharp left. Here leave it at the stile and ascend the field to a stile. Cross the next field to a wall on your right and walk beside it as you descend gently to a footbridge. Continue beside the wall before curving right to a stile with a house on your left. Descend the track/drive which curves left to the road junction in Rudyard beside the Poachers Tavern. Descend the road to the railway bridge, 1/4 mile and turn right up the track to the car park.

REMEMBER
AND
OBSERVE
THE
COUNTRY CODE

 Enjoy the countryside and respect its life and work.

 Guard against all risk of fire.

Fasten all gates.

Keep your dogs under close control.

 Keep to public paths across farmland.

Use gates and stiles to cross fences, hedges and walls.

  Leave livestock, crops and machinery alone.

Take your litter home - pack it in; pack it out.

Help to keep all water clean.

 Protect wildlife, plants and trees.

 Take special care on country roads.

CALDON CANAL & KNYPERSLEY RESERVOIR - 20 MILES

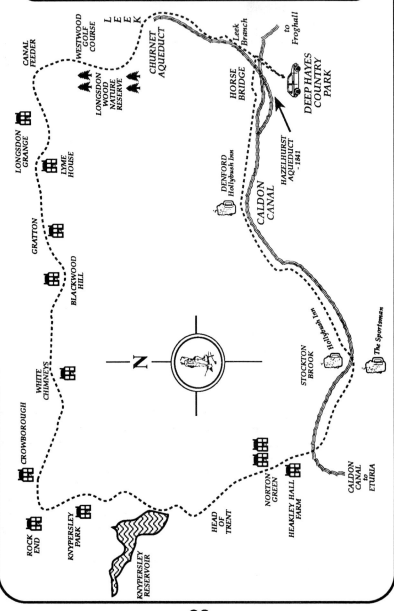

L E E K

WESTWOOD GOLF COURSE

CANAL FEEDER

LONGSDON WOOD NATURE RESERVE

CHURNET AQUEDUCT

Leek Branch

to Froghall

HORSE BRIDGE

DEEP HAYES COUNTRY PARK

LONGSDON GRANGE

LYME HOUSE

DENFORD Hollybush Inn

HAZELHURST AQUEDUCT - 1841

GRATTON

CALDON CANAL

BLACKWOOD HILL

N

WHITE CHIMNEYS

Hollybush Inn

The Sportsman

CROWBOROUGH

STOCKTON BROOK

ROCK END

KNYPERSLEY PARK

HEAD OF TRENT

NORTON GREEN

HEAKLEY HALL FARM

CALDON CANAL to ETURIA

KNYPERSLEY RESERVOIR

CALDON CANAL & KNYPERSLEY RESERVOIR
- 20 MILES
- allow 7 hours

Deep Hayes Country Park Car Park · Horse Bridge · Caldon Canal (Leek Branch) · Churnet Aqueduct · Canal Feeder · Longsdon Wood · Longsdon Grange · Lyme House · Gratton · Blackwood Hill · White Chimneys · Crowborough · Rock End · Knypersley Reservoir Head of Trent · Canal Feeder · Norton Green · Heakley Hall Farm · Caldon Canal · Deep Hayes Country Park.

· O.S. 1:25,000 Pathfinder Series Sheet No. SJ 85/95 Kidsgrove and Leek.

· Deep Hayes Country Park. Grid Ref. SJ963534.

· Nothing en route until the latter stages · Hollybush Inn & The Sportsman, Stockton Brook, just north of the Caldon Canal. Hollybush Inn, Denford by the Caldon Canal.

ABOUT THE WALK - Longer than many in this book but a walk of great quality exploring the Caldon Canal and its feeder canals from Rudyard and Knypersley Reservoirs. The crossing of the high country between the two follows little used rights of way, but all the stiles are there. The views as you cross are extensive to Mow Cop in Cheshire and all over northern Staffordshire. You reach the jewel of Knypersley Reservoir at the half way point before descending its feeder canal to the Caldon Canal. Here you have a level five mile walk back to your start amidst tranquil surroundings and passing two inns. For me this walk is a truly outstanding day out in the countryside to the west of Leek.

If you want to extend this walk by a further 5 miles you can link it with the Biddulph Moor walk!

WALKING INSTRUCTIONS - From the car park return to the minor road at the entrance to the Country Park, and walk over the bridge over the Caldon Canal - this is where you will returning to in seven hours time! Continue along the road ascending gently to the Leek arm of the Caldon Canal. Just before the bridge and on the righthand side of "Woodvale" house, descend to the canal and walk under the bridge. You now keep to the righthand side of the canal for more than mile to the Leek Tunnel. Here ascend the steps and walk over the tunnel on the well defined path and descend back to the canal. Continue beside the canal for almost 3/4 mile to the Churnet Aqueduct, built by John Rennie in 1801. Here the canal abruptly ends. Bear left through a stile on the lefthand side of the aqueduct and follow the canal feeder - not the River Churnet. The path is well used and in just over 1/4 mile reach the A53 road.

Cross the A53 to a stile by the path sign - "Rudyard 2 1/4 miles." The path is well defined and stiled as you continue with the canal feeder on your immediate left for the next 2 miles. At first on your right is the Westwood golf course, then you enter Longsdon Wood, a nature reserve. When you leave the boundary of the reserve 1 1/2 miles away, you turn sharp left and cross a footbridge and ascend steeply with a stone wall on your left. Reach a stone stile and continue beside the wall to another stile. You have superb views from here to Rudyard Reservoir. Through this turn left and keep the wall on your left for a while before bearing right to a gate and stile near the righthand corner of the narrow field. Now heading almost due westward you keep the wall on your left and cross the level fields, using stiles to a minor road. On your right is Longsdon Grange. At the road turn right and walk past a ruined house on your left. Just after on your left is a small gate. Go through this and keep the field boundary on your right as you descend to a stile. Continue descending to another and follow the lefthand track to the lefthand edge of Lyme House Farm. The right of way is little used and you may have to manoeuvre yourself around several farm trailers to reach the stile!

Cross the road beyond to your left to another stile; the slopes on your left are covered with woodland - Bradshaw Plantation. This next right of way is little used but well stiled to Gratton just over a mile away. Basically keep the field boundary on your right for two fields to a stile. After this turn right and keep the field edge and stream on your right to another stile. Cross this and walk to your left inbetween two streams for 20 yards. There is no footbridge here so you will have jump across the narrow rivelet. Cross the subsequent field to a stile well to the left of the solitary house - Blake Meadows. Bear slightly left in the next field aiming for the footbridge over Horton Brook. Go through a stone stile just after and here the rights of way divide. Take the lefthand one -

although it is not defined - and go through the gate - and diagonally cross the field to its lefthand side to a solitary stone pillar where there is a metal stile. Pass through this and bear right and ascend the field beside the righthand boundary and passing under the electricity power lines. At the top of the field turn left and follow the track to a stile and on past the buildings of Gratton Hall on your left, and reach a magnificent stile made out of old grindstones.

Turn left then right - signposted Lask Edge 2 miles - and follow the country lane down to a cross roads. Keep straight ahead and continue on the lane for 1/2 mile to where it turns sharp left, with another lane on your right and a farm drive straight ahead. Walk up this farm drive to Small Lane Farm. Keep straight ahead through the farmyard to a gate and continue on the walled track to another gate and road from Blackwood Hill. Bear right along the road and in 1/4 mile pass "White Shaw " house dated 1922 on your right. Just after turn left on the track/drive to White Chimneys Farm. Keep to the right of the farm to a stile and continue along the field boundary on your right to a gate and another beside a minor road. Turn left along it towards Cowall Moor. In just over 1/4 mile where the road bears left pass Gadshill Bank House dated 1899, on your left. Just after turn right along a drive past a house to a gate. Continue ahead in the field to a stone stile and maintain this direction until you gain a road near Crowborough Farm less than 1/2 mile away. The next stile is on your left in the wall and by a holly tree. Continue ahead passing wooden posts on your left to another stone stile. At the end of the next field is a gate gap. Continue to a gate and stile beyond and reach the road. This is another of those well stiled but little used rights of way.

Continue ahead along the road to a cross roads and turn left and pass a well dated 1896 on your left. All the time the impressive rock outcrops - Wicken Stones - can be seen ahead. Follow the road (Crowborough Road) down, around and up to Rock End. At the road junction keep left and follow the road for 50 yards to opposite a cattle grid and turn left along Lodge Barn Road. 1/4 mile along here keep straight ahead on the track as you enter pine trees, heather and rocky outcrops on your left. Just past two outcrops you pass a small pool on your left. Just after turn right at a stile and follow the defined path keeping beside the fence on your left, as you descend to two more stiles. After the second one turn left and soon descend again to the edge of Knypersley Reservoir. Turn left along the track and walk around the reservoir to the road beside Poolside Cottage on your left.

Turn right along the dam wall for a few yards before turning left at the footpath sign - Norton Green. Descend the steps to the pond of Knypersley Mill. Bear right at the bottom to a stile and pass the pond overflow on your left and reach another stile. After this you swing left following and keeping close to the "Head of Trent". At first it is on your left but you cross a footbridge and it is now on your right. In a 1/3 mile you reach a minor road from Ridgeway.Cross the road and as signed - Norton Green - continue ahead keeping the canal feeder on your immediate left. Don't follow the stream on your right. You follow this for just over 1/2 mile to the next road. Cross to your right to a stile and path sign. Continue beside the field boundary on your right to three stiles. Ahead can be seen the fourth one. Keep the canal feeder on your left to end of the next field with a stile from another right of way on your left. Follow the field round to your left to another stile and continue beside the canal feeder for a few yards to a field gap and "footbridge". Cross this and turn right keeping the field boundary on your right to reach a housing estate in Norton Green. Continue ahead along the tarmaced path past the houses on your left to the main road B5051. On your right is a shop! Continue ahead with the green on your right following the path to another road. Go straight across and walk along the drive to Heakley Hall Farm. Walk around the righthand side of the farm on the track to reach bridge No.22 of the Caldon Canal. Cross the bridge and turn left and follow the towpath on the righthand side of the canal.

Follow the canal for the next mile passing milepost -Eturia 6 miles, Uttoxeter 24 miles. Just after pass a drawbridge and 1/4 mile later the locks - 5,6,7,8 - at Stockton Brook. If you ascend the road bridge, the Hollybush Inn is just a few yards to your left. Continue beside the canal passing Greenway Hall Golf Course on your right. At the road bridge here cross over and continue along the lefthand side of the canal. 3/4 mile later cross the footbridge over the entrance to the Stoke Boat Club marina. Two miles later the canal divides. Keep to the lefthand one and descend the locks. The one to the right is the Leek branch whose upper part you followed at the start of the walk. Continue past the locks and in 1/4 mile walk under the Hazelhurst Aqueduct built in 1841, carrying the Leek branch. Just after reach Denford and the canal side pub - The Hollybush Inn. Beside it is the canal milepost - Eturia 10 miles, Uttoxeter 20 miles. Not far to go now, continue beside the canal for less than 1/2 mile to the road bridge you walked over at the start. Walk through it before turning left to the stile and gaining the road. Turn left and walk up the drive back to Deep Hayes Car Park.

THE HIKER'S CODE

❀ *Hike only along marked routes - do not leave the trail.*

❀ *Use stiles to climb fences; close gates.*

❀ *Camp only in designated campsites.*

❀ *Carry a light-weight stove.*

❀ *Leave the trail cleaner than you found it.*

❀ *Leave flowers and plants for others to enjoy.*

❀ *Keep dogs on a leash.*

❀ *Protect and do not disturb wildlife.*

❀ *Use the trail at your own risk.*

❀ *Leave only your thanks and footprints - take nothing but photographs.*

ONECOTE AND COOMBES VALLEY - 18 MILES

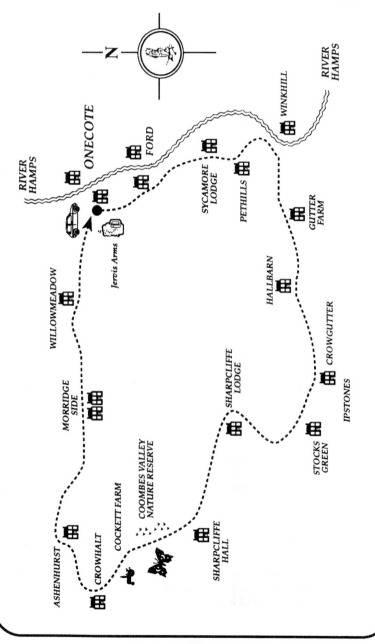

N

RIVER HAMPS

WINKHILL

RIVER HAMPS

ONECOTE

FORD

SYCAMORE LODGE

PETHILLS

GUTTER FARM

Jervis Arms

HALLBARN

WILLOWMEADOW

CROWGUTTER

IPSTONES

MORRIDGE SIDE

SHARPCLIFFE LODGE

STOCKS GREEN

COOMBES VALLEY NATURE RESERVE

ASHENHURST

CROWHALT

COCKETT FARM

SHARPCLIFFE HALL

ONECOTE AND COOMBES VALLEY
- 18 MILES
- allow 6 to 7 hours.

- Onecote - Ford - Sycamore Lodge - Pethills - Winkhill - Gutter Farm - Hallbarn - Ipstones - Crowgutter - Stocks Green - Sharpcliffe Lodge - Sharpcliffe Hall - Coombes Valley Nature Reserve - Cockett Farm - Crowhalt - Ashenhurst - Morridge Side - Willowmeadow - Onecote.

 - No official one at Onecote.

 - 1:25,000 Outdoor Leisure Map - The White Peak - west sheet.

 - Jervis Arms, Onecote.

ABOUT THE WALK - The first time I did this walk was on a New Years day - as a first footing. The day started fine but by the time I was reaching Sharpcliffe the heavens had opened and I was soon soaked to the skin; but I enjoyed it! I finally found a moments respite in the hide in the Coombes Valley. Here I unearthed my traditional bottle of wine, chicken leg and large hunk of Christmas cake. One eaten I continued in the rain, now being whipped up by a strong wind. Descending to Onecote was a nightmare in the dark and rain and I lost the stiles. But of no consequence it was a great day out and I was soon back home in a hot bath! I have since walked it in the height of summer but it wasn't the same - it was too easy!

The route first takes you down the Hamps valley to Ford and onto Winkhill before heading westwards across country to Ipstones. Here you head north westerly to the Coombes Valley Nature Reserve before aiming eastwards to Onecote via Morridge Side. The whole walk is well stiled and signed but many of the paths are little used and constant checking on the map will help ensure you are on the right path.

WALKING INSTRUCTIONS - In Onecote walk southwards along the B5053 road past the Jervis Arms and a few yards later on your left is the footpath sign and stile. Soon reach a stile and footbridge. For the next 3/4 mile keep the field boundary on your immediate right - mostly a fence - and you will come to all the stiles or gates. After the seventh field the path angles left slightly as you descend to Banktop and Ford. Turn left to the main road in Ford and opposite the road bridge turn right along the road. 50 yards later turn left into Ford Farm and at the end of the buildings reach a gate. Continue ahead on a track keeping close to the field boundary on your right, crossing a stream and passing through three more gates to reach the crossroads of tracks at Sycamore Lodge. Keep straight ahead to a stile and continue on the track as it maintains its high elevation above the River Hamps. In just over 1/2 mile gain the minor road opposite Pethills. Turn left and descend to the River Hamps. At the stile and footpath sign turn right beside it, keeping the river on your left. In a 1/3 mile gain the A523 at Winkhill.

Cross the A523 road to a minor road and in a few yards turn right at a stile with the house - Green Acres just ahead. Don't ascend the field to a barn keep left first past the house garden then to the far righthand corner of the field where there is a stile. Turn right then left and keep the wall on your left to another stile. Afterwards descend the fields aiming diagonally right to reach a minor road opposite Gutter Farm. Cross to the right to a stile and continue past the farm on your left to kissing gates and railway line. Cross over and keep the wall on your left for the next two fields. After the second field you begin ascending more steeply. Cross a wall with no stile and reach a stile in the wall corner, with the farm Hallbarn will to your right. Keep the wall on your left for a few yards before bearing right slightly to a stile and by keeping in this almost due west direction you will come to the stiles. Cross the track to Hallbarn and gain a gate before the minor road at the crest of Ipstones Edge. Turn right then left and at the start of a track on your left, bear right and angle westwards down the fields, guided by stiles. In less then 1/2 mile bear left and continue descending and gain a track. Descend this with a wall on your left to reach a stile and road opposite Crowgutter Farm.

Turn right along the lane - Park Lane - to the B5053 road on the outskirts of Ipstones - Stocks Green - beside Toll Bar Cottage. Go straight across the road and follow the stiled right of way. After five stiles turn right (not sharp right) - now heading due north - on a well stiled path. In just over 1/2 mile gain the track from Sharpcliffe Lodge, via a stile. Turn right along the track and at the lodge turn left following the drive to Sharpcliffe Hall nearly a mile away. The walk through here is particularly attractive being wooded and the gritstone

- Sharpcliffe Rocks - on your right. Walk past the farm buildings on your left and keep on the track on the righthand side of Sharpcliffe Hall. Pass Cottage Farm on your left and reach a gate. Soon after enter the Coombes Valley Nature Reserve and follow the distinct path as it descends to a footbridge and hide on your right.

Cross the footbridge and follow the path to your right that ascends out of the reserve. Don't bear right to a minor road but keep ahead and cross two more fields before the road. Turn left along it and just past Cockett Farm turn right at the stile. Angle left across the field to a stile and cross the next to a stile on the left of a wood. Here join a track and follow it past Crowhalt to a stile and continue along the field edge to another stile and onto Finney Lane. Once here you now turn eastwards and basically keep in that direction all the way back to Onecote - 4 1/2 miles away! Turn right - eastwards - to a stile and another. After this keep the hedge on your right as you cross several fields to Ashenhurst, 1/3 mile away. Just after gain a crossroads of paths by a sign and stile. Turn right onto a track and in 1/4 mile reach "Fernleigh". Keep to the left and continue on a track that curves round to your right and 1/4 mile later it curves again. Partway round the curve is a stile and leave the track here and continue first with a wall on your left then fence as you cross the fields to the railway line. Cross this and two stiles later gain the A523 road at Morridge Side.

Turn right then left and begin the last ascent of the day. In 1/4 mile turn right then left at the end of the lane and continue ascending to your right up a track, which is well footpath signed. After passing the third field on your left turn left at a stile - a solitary tree can be seen ahead. Ascend more steeply now aiming for the top righthand corner of the field where there is a stile. Keep the field boundary on your right as you curve round to your right and gain a track which you follow to the crest of the hill to a stile and minor road - the boundary of the Peak National Park. Cross to a stile on your right and go diagonally right across the top of the field before descending to the righthand side of Willowmeadow. Cross another field before bearing left and keeping the field boundary on your right for two fields. Well through the next field turn right to the bottom righthand corner and continue close to the stream, as you descend, on your left as you aim for the lefthand side of Onecote church. Turn right along the lane back into Onecote and the Jervis Arms Inn!

BUTTERTON AND
RIVER HAMPS - 12 MILES

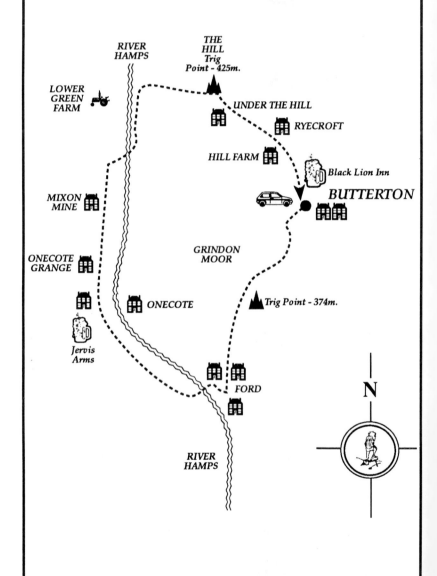

RIVER HAMPS

THE HILL Trig Point - 425m.

LOWER GREEN FARM

UNDER THE HILL

RYECROFT

HILL FARM

Black Lion Inn

BUTTERTON

MIXON MINE

GRINDON MOOR

ONECOTE GRANGE

ONECOTE

Trig Point - 374m.

Jervis Arms

FORD

RIVER HAMPS

N

BUTTERTON
&
RIVER HAMPS
- 12 MILES
- allow 4 to 5 hours

- *Butterton - Grindon Moor - Ford - River Hamps - Onecote - Onecote Grange - River Hamps - Mixon Mine - Lower Green Farm - The Hill, 425 metres - Under the Hill - Ryecroft - Hole - Hill Farm - Butterton.*

- *1:25,000 Outdoor Leisure Map - The White Peak - West Sheet.*

- *No official one in Butterton.*

- *Black Lion Inn, Butterton. Jervis Arms, Onecote.*

ABOUT THE WALK - I have often written about walks in this area of Staffordshire/Peak District simply because it is an outstanding and little used area. The views, especially from The Hill, are exceptional and I still consider it to be among the top three vantage points in the National Park. The walk is a meandering one along good paths and tracks, with gentle ascents and descents - except The Hill! Ford is a delightful little hamlet with flowing river; Onecote is bigger with a highly recommended inn! and Butterton is bigger still and full of interest and worth exploring in its own right. I never tire of hiking this area and I am sure that you too will enjoy the high country walking here.

WALKING INSTRUCTIONS - Starting from the Black Lion Inn in Butterton, descend the narrow road all the way down the impressive ford, crossed by two footpath bridges. Ascend the road beyond a short distance to the first farm drive (to Coxon Green) on your right. Turn right then left to the corner of the upper farm where there is a stile on your side of the building. Ascend the stile and keep the field edge on your right and cross three stiles to reach the righthand side of another farm. Continue ahead to the next stile and keep the lefthand side of the field to a stile in the top lefthand corner of the field. In the lefthand field is a solitary barn. Continue with the fence on your right to another stile. Ignore a track and slightly to your right is a stile and road beyond ; to your left is a solitary tree and further away a trig point - 347 metres.

Cross the minor road from Grindon to your right to another stile. Cross the field aiming for the lefthand side of Sheldon Farm. Keep the wall on your right to a stile and path sign. Ascend the stile and turn left keeping the wall on your left now to another stile. After this the field boundary - a fence - is now on your right as you descend on a track to Ford. After 1/2 mile you walk through a farm and reach the road. Turn right and walk past the houses and where the road turns left and crosses the River Hamps keep ahead to the path sign - "Onecote". Keep right; not up the private drive and walk around the lefthand side of some buildings to a track. Follow this round to a gate with the River Hamps on your left. Continue on the track and where it divides keep right. 1/4 mile later the track turns sharp right to Bullclough. Leave the track and continue ahead to a stile. Continue crossing the next field to a stile and 1/4 mile later at the end of a small slope on your right is a white post/ footpath sign. Continue ahead bearing slightly to your right to keep the field boundary on your left and reach another white post and stile. Over this bear left to a stile, footbridge and pathsign beside the B5053 road. Turn left and enter Onecote and pass the Jervis Arms on your right.

Just past the inn turn right along the minor road past the church and in 1/4 mile turn right along the drive to Onecote Grange, as footpath signed - "Mixon Mines 1 1/4 miles; Mermaid 3 1/4 miles." Approaching the Grange turn left to pass between it and farm buildings on your left to reach a gate. Through this continue on the track for the next 1 1/4 miles to Mixon Mine; on your right and below you is the River Hamps. At Mixon Mine Farm bear right as signed - Mermaid - and follow the stiled path to another stile. The path is defined as you cross the fields to a former reservoir. Reach a stile beyond it and continue across two more fields to a signed path junction. Turn right and descend to the River Hamps and footbridge. Cross this and turn left to walk above the river and small dam on your left. Little over 1/4 mile you approach Lower Green Farm but don't cross the wall - you turn right as footpath signed - "Elkstone". The sign states that - *"Naturists may be ahead!"* This is not why I walk here and I have never seen any Aphrodite!

You now ascend keeping the wall on your left and gain several stiles as you climb "The Hill." At the top cross a minor road via stiles and gain the trig point, 425 metres. The view over the area to the Mermaid and Manifold Valley can only be described as fantastic. Keep straight ahead and descend steeply to the lefthand side of Under the Hill, ascending two stiles to the farm road. Cross this to your right to the immediate left of the building, to another stile, and continue descending with the field boundary on your left. En route pass water troughs. At the bottom of the field turn right and keep the field edge on your left and descend to a footbridge. Ascend the otherside aiming for the lefthand side of Ryecroft. Here find two stiles as you bear right through pine trees to a stile and footbridge. Keep the fence on your left to another stile before aiming for the righthand side of Hole. Walk around the house on the track and continue on it for about 150 yards to a pathsign - "Butterton." Here leave the track and follow a path contouring around the fields. The path is defined and well stiled and in 1/4 mile becomes a track as you approach Hill Farm. Keep to the right of the farm by ascending a small sunken path. Keep ahead to a stile, gate and "Butterton" path sign. Continue ascending with a wall on your left to a stile, footpath sign and B5053 road.

Cross over to another stile and path sign and follow the path with the wall on your right for two fields. Cross two small fields and reach a minor road to Butterton. Turn right and in 50 yards left at a stile and keep the wall on your left for two fields before turning right and gaining Butterton village via Croft Head Farm. All the time Butterton church acts as a useful guide. Turn left and left again to reach the Black Lion Inn.

ALSTONEFIELD - 12 MILES

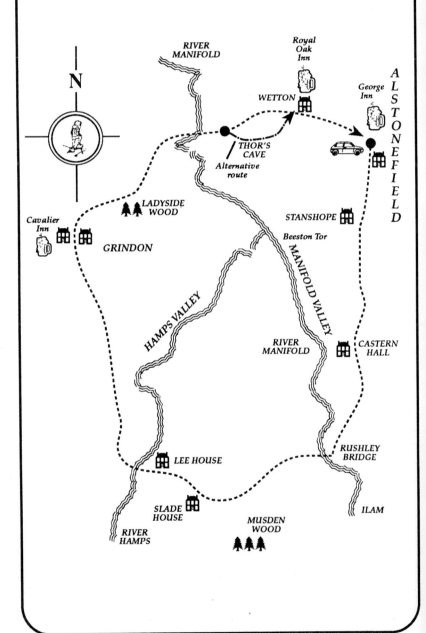

ALSTONEFIELD
- 12 MILES
- allow 4 to 5 hours.

- Alstonefield - Stanshope - Castern Hall - Rushley Bridge - Slade House - Lee House - Hamps Valley - Deepdale - Grindon - Ladyside Wood - Thor's Cave - Wetton - Alstonefield.

- 1:25,000 Outdoor Leisure Map - The White Peak - West Sheet.

- Alstonefield. Grid Ref. SK132557.

- George Inn, Alstonefield; Cavalier Inn, Grindon; and Royal Oak Inn, Wetton. There are also tea rooms in Alstonefield, Hamps Valley and Wetton.

ABOUT THE WALK - Rather than descend the dales and valleys this walk is more adventurous - cutting across them! The reward is stunning distant views and sights of familiar places from different angles. You will ascend and descend over 2,000 feet as you walk round. I did this walk one bright spring day when all the daffodils, primroses, violets, and wood anemones were out and was a magical time....until near the end - it sheeted with rain and I was soaked. Have a good walk as you explore the high country between the Hamps and Manifold Valleys.

WALKING INSTRUCTIONS - Turn right out of the car park and right again immediately up the track from the "coach" park. At the top turn right to the Hopedale/ Wetton road junction with the school opposite - you return back to here. Turn left for a few yards before turning sharp left along a track on your left passing a house on your right at the start. In less than a 1/4 mile the track turns sharp right. Leave it here at the stile and descend with the wall on your right. Follow the wall round to your right to a stile and continue descending to a stile, footpath sign and road. Cross the road and ascend the track - footpath signed. In 1/2 mile reach Stanshope Hall and road. Turn left along the road for 1/4 mile to a stile and path sign on your right. Cross the field to its top righthand corner where there is a stile. Continue gently ascending to another stile and footpath crossroads. Keep straight ahead with the wall on your right and at the fourth stile keep the wall on your left to gain a stile on the edge of Castern Farm. Turn right along farm track and at the top, as path signed, turn left beside the wall to another stile. Descend the field to a stile and reach the farm drive - you have partially encircled the farm. Continue down the drive and passing Castern Hall on your right. Descend the drive and at the first bend bear left to a stile and descend, cutting a bend in the road, to steps and road. Cross over and continue descending following a track to the left to a stile. Cross the subsequent field to a solitary stone stile and at the end of the next field gain the lefthand side of Rushley Bridge, via a stile and path sign.

Turn right and cross the River Manifold and walk up the road to the junction and turn right. After a few yards turn left at the stile and footpath sign and ascend the field to a stile. Cross the next to a large ladder stile. Bear right and keep the wall on your right and soon follow a track beside it. At the end of the field bear left going diagonally across the field to the top righthand corner where there is a stile - you should have seen it on the skyline. Turn left and keep the wall on your left for the next 1/2 mile as you pass a barn on your left, a Limekiln on your right, and another barn on your left before reaching Shady House. Descend to the drive/track and turn right it. Two fields later pass some ponds on your right and reach a gate. Turn left, leaving the track and cross the field to the far lefthand corner; in the final stages keep the wall on your left. Here gain a stile, path sign and minor road. Cross over to another stile and descend first with the wall on your right and later on your left, as you walk through sparse woodland and gain the lefthand side of Lee House. Cross the footbridge over the River Hamps to the Manifold Track.

Cross over to a kissing gate and turn right to a gate and track. Follow the track through woodland and beyond past a barn on your right. The path is defined as you reach a small gate. Continue ascending diagonally up the fields guided by the small gates to a lane. Turn right along it to a gate. Continue along the track to a farm and walk through the farmyard to a gate and descend the track directly infront of you, down into Deepdale. Ascend to your right for a few yards before turning left keeping the wall on your left. After two fields reach a track and follow this into Grindon, 1/2 mile away, taking the righthand fork in the final stages to reach the White House on your right. Turn right then left around the "green" and before the row of houses turn right, as footpath signed. Partway through the field reach a path sign and bear right and descend to a footbridge and stile. Continue on the well defined path as you descend into Ladyside Wood, National Trust property. The views of Thor's Cave are particularly attractive here. Descend to the Manifold Track.

Cross the track to a footbridge and cross the River Manifold. You now start your last major ascent! You have a choice; either keep to the lefthand path and ascend the shallow vale to Wetton or take the path to your right and ascend to Thor's Cave and then along a concessionary path along a lane to Wetton. Both reach Wetton at the same point. Take the lefthand road into Wetton village, passing the church on your right. Follow the road round to your right to the Royal Oak Inn. Here turn left along the road and just past Town End Farm (the last house on your left) , at a minor road, go through the stile on your right and descend the field to the bottom righthand corner to a stile. Continue to the next ones curving gently to the right and reach a walled track. Follow this to the road beside Brook Lodge. Turn left and in about 50 yards on your right is the stile and path sign. Turn right keeping the hedge on your left to a stile in it. Cross this to another and basically keep straight ahead to a minor road. Cross this via stiles and ascend the fields on a defined path and over the brow the hill walk past the football field of Alstonefield School and gain the road beside it. Turn right then left and descend back to the car park.

FOUR STAFFORDSHIRE VILLAGES - 8 MILES

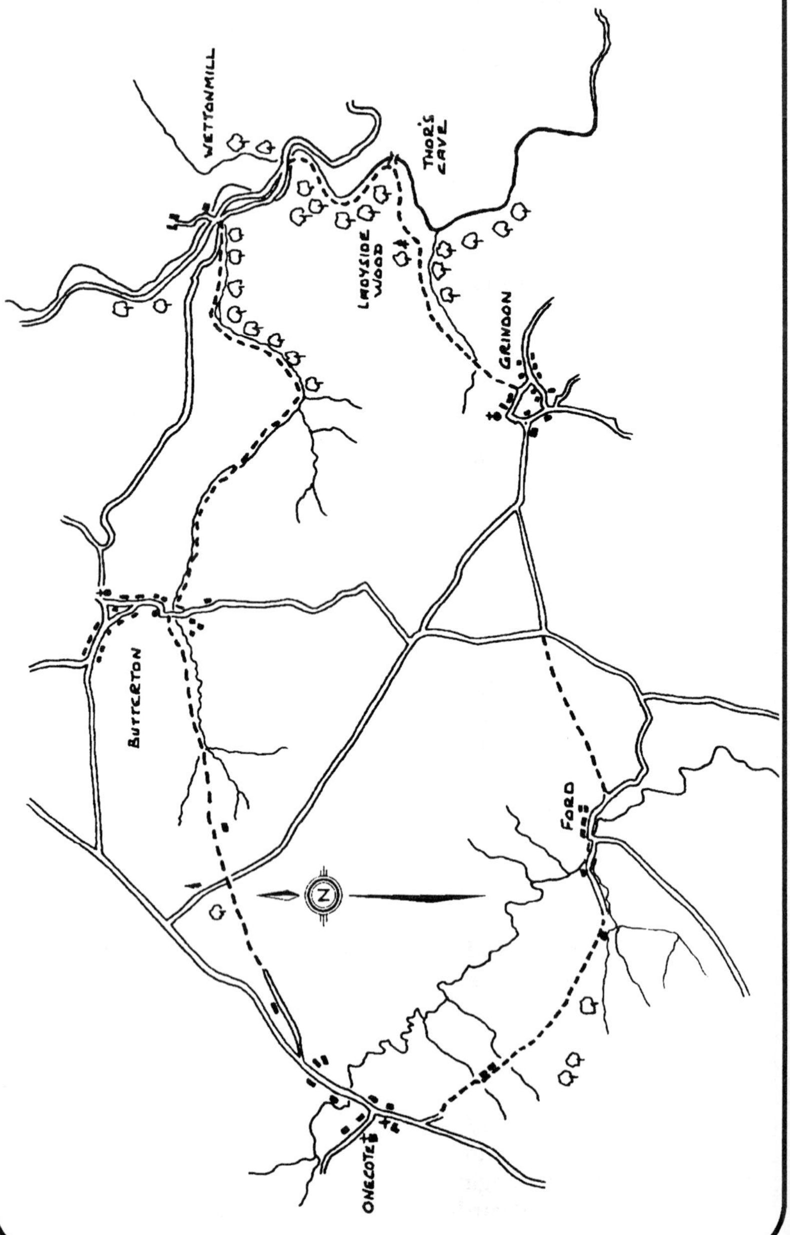

WETTONMILL

THOR'S CAVE

LADYSIDE WOOD

GRINDON

BUTTERTON

FORD

ONECOTE

FOUR STAFFORDSHIRE
VILLAGES- 8 miles - allow 3 hours.

- *Wettonmill—Thor's Cave—Ladyside Wood—Grindon—Ford—Banktop—Onecote—Home Farm—The Twist—Butterton Ford—Hoe Brook —Wettonmill.*

 : *Wettonmill. Grid Ref. SK095562.*

 O.S. 1:25,000 Outdoor Leisure Map—The White Peak - West sheet.

- *Cavalier Inn, Grindon; Jervis Arms, Onecote; Black Lion Inn, Butterton.*

ABOUT THE WALK - The walk begins from one of the Peak District's most scenic valleys—the Manifold. After just over half a mile of walking in the valley the route takes you into unspoilt but beautiful countryside to the west. The walk visits four villages on the limestone plateau, providing extensive views and glimpses of many attractive and interesting buildings. At three of the villages—Grindon, Onecote and Butterton—are inns and although only short the route makes an ideal Sunday walk to savour an area of the National Park not visited by many.

WALKING INSTRUCTIONS - From the car park head almost eastwards and follow the single track road past the campsite on your right. Wettonmill, just over the bridge on your left, serves teas and snacks and makes a perfect end to the walk. A 1/4 mile later, where the road turns left to ascend to Wetton, keep straight ahead and follow the tarmac surface of the old light railway which operated here until the early 1930s. About 1/4 mile along here you near the footbridge on your left for the path to Thor's Cave. Here you turn right through the wooden stile and begin your gentle ascent to Grindon village 3/4 mile away. After 100 yards you go through a gap in a crumbled wall and bear left following a distinct path through trees. Follow this graded path and where it bends to your right follow it to open country. Keep to the left-hand side of the field and when you reach a cluster of pine trees on your left, turn left and continue traversing round a valley side through Ladyside Wood. After half a mile you reach a concrete water trough. The stile is on the immediate left-hand side. Keep straight ahead as you cross an open field towards Grindon. As you near the village you keep a wall on your immediate right to reach a short lane with a footpath sign. As you approach Grindon look behind you for this is a magnificent viewpoint for Thor's Cave and the village of Wetton.

Upon reaching Grindon turn right towards the church which was built in 1848. Turn left in front of it and at the next road junction shortly afterwards, turn right (the Cavalier Inn is down the road on your left) and walk along the road past Crown Farm on your left. After 1/4 mile turn left following the signposted road—Waterhouses 3 1/2 miles. Just over 1/4 mile along this road you reach a T-junction. Opposite on the right can be seen the stile. The path line is not obvious but keep the field boundary on your left before crossing an open field to another stile. Now you keep the field boundary on your immediate right as you descend using the stiles to the road on the southern edge of Ford village. As you descend you have extensive views over the, area, especially to Onecote, your next objective. At the road turn right into Ford village, and what a delightful village it is, with the River Hamps running through it. Cross the road bridge on your left and immediately turn right along the lane to Banktop. Walk past the house on your right and keep on the lane. Upon reaching the next building on your left keep straight ahead and ascend the wooden stile on the right of the metal gate. You are now walking along a grass bridleway, although for the next 1/4 mile there is little to be seen of it on the ground and you should keep the field boundary on your right. The bridleway then becomes more obvious as you reach a gate and walled track beyond. A further half mile brings you to the B5053 road on the southern outskirts of Onecote village. Turn right; as you walk through the village you pass the Jervis Arms on your left.

Keep on the road (B5053) for about 1/4 mile and just past the entrance to Onecote Old Hall Farm, turn right up a tarmac lane passing Home Farm on your left. Shortly afterwards the lane turns sharp right. You keep straight ahead and use the wooden stile. The path from here is not obvious but basically keep the electricity poles on your immediate right. Where they turn sharp left keep straight ahead to a wooden stile. Beyond this you have a field of heather to walk across to a minor road over Grindon Moor. Cross the road to the stile on the left-hand side of the gate and descend a farm track passing Twistgreen on your right. For the remainder of the walk you will be descending. At the end of the track, with a farm building on your right, you aim for the stiles and path in front of a cottage as you continue dropping to the ford at Butterton. This section of the path is fascinating with the very narrow strip fields. You have a dozen to cross and all the stiles can be seen quite clearly. In the final stages you walk down a walled path to the lane in the bottom of Butterton village. The Black Lion Inn dated 1782 is just up this lane on your left.

Cross the ford in Butterton and walk up the road on your right. After about 100 yards use the stile on the left of the gate on your left and descend directly to Hoo Brook and a limestone stile. This almost brings you back to where you were five minutes ago but this is the correct way and a right-of-way. For the next half mile you keep the brook on your immediate left-hand side; there are stiles all the way. After half a mile a stream comes in from your right and there is a stile here. The right-of-way then crosses to the other side of the brook and you continue descending the left-hand side with the brook on your right. There is no stile here on the other side of the river so you have to cross the barbed wire fence. Soon afterwards you reach a stile. A 1/2 mile later you approach a footbridge on your right. Again there should be a stile here in order that you can continue down the dale on the left of the brook but there isn't so you have to climb a stone wall. After this there are stiles all the way for the final half mile back to the road in front of Wettonmill. It is a shame that two stiles are missing on this section from Butterton but don't be put off for it is a good walk. Now back to your starting point—why not slip across the bridge for a refreshing cup of tea?

ILAM ROCK - 8 MILES

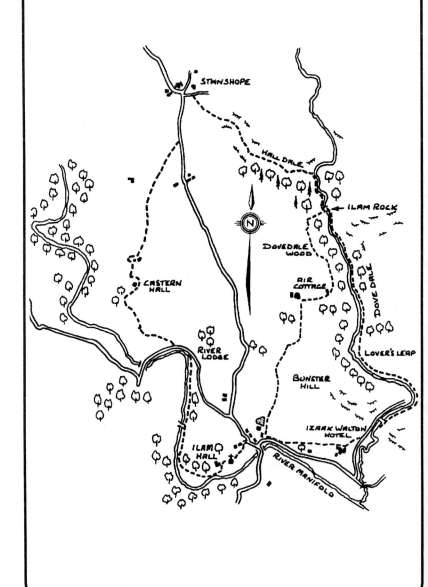

ILAM ROCK
- 8 miles
- allow 3 hours.

• • • - *Ilam Hall—River Manifold—River Lodge— Castern Hall—Stanshope—Hall Dale—Ilam Rock—Dovedale—Izaak Walton Hotel—Ilam Hall.*

Alternative route - 7 miles overall - *Ilam Rock—Dovedale Wood—Air Cottage—Bunster Hill—Ilam Hall*

 -Ilam Hall & Dove Dale.

 - O.S. 1:25,000 Outdoor Leisure Map—The White Peak - west sheet.

 - Izaak Walton Hotel.

ABOUT THIS WALK - Starting from Ilam this walk briefly touches the River Manifold before climbing out of the valley to two architectural delights. From Stanshope the route takes you down Hall Dale to Dovedale and Ilam Rock. Here you have a choice of routes. You can take the longer but more normal route and descend Dovedale to the stepping stones and follow the path across the fields back to Ilam. Alternatively you can take the shorter route and ascend steeply out of Dovedale and reach Ilam via the slopes of Bunster Hill. Either way you have here a splendid walk amidst some of the finest countryside in the Peak District.

WALKING INSTRUCTIONS - From Ilam Hall car park walk to the end of the gravel surface and descend the steps to the path close to the River Manifold and follow it round to your right. Just round the corner here the river 'bubbles' up and is known as the Bubble Holes.

During the summer months the Manifold disappears underground down a swallet at Wettonmill eight miles upstream and re-appears here. A little further and on your right is the Battle Stone, found in an Ilam house last century and part of a Saxon cross. Next you walk along a walled path known as Paradise Walk. At the end is a footbridge and path across the River Manifold to near Musden Grange. Don't cross the bridge but keep straight ahead and use a metal stile and continue walking up a distinct path with the river on your left. This is a private footpath but the public are allowed to use it provided that when they reach River Lodge, 1/3 mile away, they put one penny in the box. The first stone of the lodge was laid on 6th May 1840, by Jemima, Countess of Montgelas.

Turn left at the lodge and walk down the single track road. After 300 yards bear right at the junction and begin ascending the road to Castern Hall. As you climb you have extensive views up the Manifold Valley to Beeston Tor. Castern Hall is a magnificent 18th century building, one of the finest in the Peak District. Follow the track in front of the building and round the back of it heading to Castern Farm. In front of the farm buildings go through the metal gate on your left and ascend to the stone stile on the right of the tree. From here climb almost due north and cross the field to the stone wall on your right, on the northern side of a walled spring. There is a stile here and once over this keep the wall on your left-hand side for the next six fields. There is little evidence of a path on the ground but at each stone wall there is a stile as you cross the fields towards Stanshope. The seventh and last field is quite large and you can see the prominent stile slightly to your right. Through this turn left and descend the road to Stanshope, 1/4 mile away.

Dominating Stanshope is a large 18th century hall. You turn right in front of it as indicated by the footpath sign— Milldale, 1 mile.' After 100 yards down this walled lane turn right at another footpath sign— 'Dovedale, I mile.' The path is defined and well stiled. After a couple of fields you begin descending Hall Dale, an imposing valley with limestone but tresses and woodland. Upon reaching the River Dove turn right and walk along its banks to the footbridge across it at Ilam Rock, a most impressive limestone pinnacle approximately 100 feet high. There are several rock climbs up it and it is reputed to have first been climbed in 1850.

At the bridge you have a choice of routes. First I will describe the more normal route down Dovedale. Cross the bridge and turn right passing Pickering Tor on your left. The next 1 1/2 miles is stunning dale walking. Soon you pass beneath Reynard's Cave, the Tissington Spires and ascend the Lover's Leap, where last century a young maiden tried to end her life. Surprisingly the bushes broke her fall and she survived! Beyond the Leap the path returns to the river and beneath the slopes of Thorpe Cloud you cross the stepping stones. Walk down the road beyond and opposite the car park 1/4 mile later turn right and follow the path across the fields, passing along the northern side of the Izaak Walton Hotel before crossing three more fields to the road on the fringe of Ilam. Turn right into Ilam to the Cross and on to the entrance gates to Ilam Hall. You can either walk to the Hall via the drive or turn left and follow the path to Ilam Church as far as the Hall.

The alternative route from Ilam Rock is as follows.

Don't cross the river, instead walk to the left-hand side of the Rock and ascend directly past it. The path line on the O.S. map shows it as a direct route but on the ground the path zig-zags its way up. It is a long climb to the top of the dale but well worth the effort. At the top the path is inside the wood and readily discernible. Turn left and follow it; as you walk along you have views down on to Dovedale and its limestone spires.

After 1/4 mile you descend beside a wall before traversing across to Air Cottage which you can see from the wall. The path is not defined but the cottage makes a good target for which to head. The view from here is exceptional. Turn right from the cottage and join a farm track and follow it to Ilamtops Farm. Upon reaching the gate and wall of the farm, turn left and walk along a walled track through a small cluster of trees. At a building on your left you should use the stile on your right into the next field but the stiles beyond that are missing. It is far better to keep straight ahead with a wall on your immediate right to a stone stile. Here turn right and begin descending the slopes of Bunster Hill with a wall on your right for the next 1/4 mile. Before reaching the road on the edge of Ilam you pass a small lake on your right. At the road you join the other path from Dovedale. Turn right to Ilam Cross and on to the Hall; part of the Hall is a National Trust Information Centre and tea and snacks are available nearby.

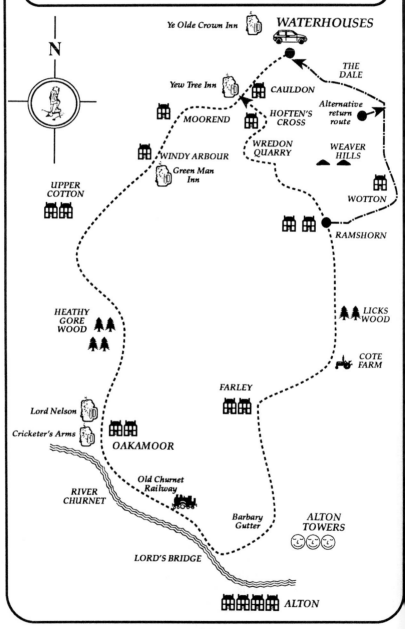

THE CHURNET VALLEY & WEAVER HILLS - 13 AND 15 MILES

N

Ye Olde Crown Inn

WATERHOUSES

THE DALE

Yew Tree Inn — CAULDON

Alternative return route

MOOREND — HOFTEN'S CROSS

WINDY ARBOUR — WREDON QUARRY — WEAVER HILLS

Green Man Inn

UPPER COTTON — WOTTON

RAMSHORN

HEATHY GORE WOOD — LICKS WOOD

COTE FARM

FARLEY

Lord Nelson

Cricketer's Arms — OAKAMOOR

Old Churnet Railway

RIVER CHURNET

Barbary Gutter — ALTON TOWERS

LORD'S BRIDGE

ALTON

THE CHURNET VALLEY & WEAVER HILLS
- 13 & 15 MILES
- allow 5 to 6 hours.

- Waterhouses Car Park - Cauldon - Moorend - Windy Harbour - Upper Cotton - Heathy Gore Wood - Cotton Bank Farm - Oakamoor - Old Churnet Railway - Lord's Bridge - Barbary Gutter - Parkhouse Farm - Farley - Cote Farm - Lick's Wood - Ramshorn - Wredon Quarry - Caldon Low - Hoften's Cross - Cauldon - Waterhouses.

Longer version - Ramshorn - Wootton - Weaver Hills - Wetside Lane - Dale Abbey Farm - Dale Lane - The Dale - Waterhouses.

- Outdoor Leisure Map 1:25,000 - The Peak District - west sheet.
- Pathfinder Series 1:25,000 - Sheet No. 04/14 - Ashbourne and the Churnet Valley.

- Waterhouses. Grid Ref. SK085502.

- Ye Olde Crown Inn, Waterhouses; Yew Tree Inn, Cauldon; The Green Man, Windy Harbour; The Lord Nelson and Cricketer's Arms, Oakamoor; The Cross Inn, Hoften's Cross.

ABOUT THE WALK - Waterhouses is usually the starting point for the River Hamps and Manifold Valley but instead of heading north into the Peak National Park you head south into more attractive scenery! The route has long been a favourite of mine passing through attractive woodland and with views of hills and valleys. You pass the spectrum of modern life - the impressive Churnet Valley and the towers and noise of Alton Towers! Shortly afterwards you are gazing into the eyes of Highland cattle and seeing a herd of red deer. The final section is a mixture of sadness and joy. First you see and pass either over or below the Weaver Hills before navigating around the limestone quarries. From Ramshorn you can either do a direct route via Wredon Quarry and Caldon Low or road walk to Wootton and walk over the hills to The Dale, one of the jewels of the Staffordshire Moorlands. Either route necessitates a road walk but a small price to pay to see such magnificent scenery. Apart from the Churnet Valley area much of the route follows little used rights of way but they are well stiled and signed.

WALKING INSTRUCTIONS - From the car park return to the road and cross over to your right to a small telephone exchange close to railway bridge. Between them is the signed footpath. Turn left up here following a tarmaced path shielded from Caldonlow Quarries for much of its length. In a 1/3 mile gain the road in the village of Cauldon and keep right at all junctions to pass the church and reach the minor road beside the Yew Tree Inn - the tree is still growing by the inn. If you return over Wredon Quarry you will return to here. Turn right up the road and in 1/4 mile turn right into Stoney Road. Follow this road for less than 1/4 mile to the start of a row of houses on your right. Here turn left through a stile and go diagonally across the field to its far end to a gate. Cross the next field to its lefthand side to a stile and continue to another on the right of a house and just after gain the road. Turn left then right almost immediately to a stile and cross the small field with the field boundary on your right and reach the A52 road. To your left is the Green Man Inn at Windy Harbour.

Cross the A52 road to your right to a stile below the road. The pathline does not exist, but keep straight ahead and when you reach a partial wall on your right bear left and descend to a stile. Cross the old railway line to another and turn right walking beside the edge of the field for a 100 yards to the line of a watercourse on your left. Follow this on its lefthand side and ascend over an embankment to a stile. Cross a rather wet and swampy wooded area to another stile and bear right down the field to a gate. Cross the next filed to a stile to the left of a solitary house. Descend the next field to a stile and minor road at Upper Cotton, with a small waterfall to your left. Turn right and in a few yards left through a gate and walk past the righthand side of a small farm via the gates and descend to a stile. Ascend the otherside and bear left to a stile and gain a track at the top of the next field just to the right of the lefthand corner, and turn left along it.

Keep on this track beside and through woodland for more than a mile. After 1/2 mile pass Cotton Bank Farm on your left and just afterwards follow the track round to your right then left. 1/4 mile later bear right then left as you leave the wood behind walking along a walled track and descend past Orchard Farm to the minor road from Oakamoor. Continue descending into Oakamoor passing the Lord Nelson Inn and Cricketers Arms at the bottom. Turn right then left immediately onto the path on the lefthand side of the River Churnet, and walk through the picnic area. Do not cross the river but keep to the track following the line of the Churnet Valley Railway - a concessionary path. This is delightful walking in woodland with the river meandering closeby.

Keep on the old line for over a mile to the first bridge - Lord's Bridge. Just before it turn left up the path to it. Don't cross it but keep left along the track through the woodland of Barbary Gutter. You soon begin ascending and pass some steps to your left ascending to a large oak tree held together with chains.

At the top before Farley Lane and a building with twin towers, cross the drive to a stile by a footpath sign - "Farley". Ascend the field past a few pine trees to a gate in the hollow below. Continue ahead along the field edge to another gate. Cross the track to Parkhouse Farm to a stile and another and cross the next field aiming to the right of a house garden which juts out into the field. Here gain a stile, steps and path sign - Alton - as you gain the road close to Farley Hall. As you ascended to here on your right is Alton Towers. Turn right then left at Farley Cottage into a small lane. In a few yards turn right onto the old road. 200 yards along here turn left upto a stile and cross the farm drive to the bottom lefthand corner of the field - beware of Highland cattle - where there is a stile. Cross to a gate and continue ahead on the farm drive to Cote Farm. Walk through the farm and down to a gate on your left by a footpath sign. Walk just inside the wood - Lick's Wood - and as guided by path signs keep just inside the wood for the next 1/3 mile. To your left you will see a herd of red deer.

Upon reaching a farm road cross over and continue ascending, as indicated by a pathsign, to a gate on your left. Go through this and keep just inside the wood to another gate and pass a cottage on your right and at the top reach a gate and farm track. Turn right past Bank End to the road junction and telephone kiosk in the hamlet of Ramshorn. Here you have to decide whether to do the shorter version described first or the longer one!

From the road junction in Ramshorn turn left and in 100 yards right through Sycamore Farm keeping the field boundary first on your right, then left, then right; it is well stiled for the first 1/3 mile then it is open fields as you aim for a gate by a track with a small coppice on your right. Cross to two more gates before bearing right and descending a field to a wooden stile. Now you ascend steeply to the edge of Wredon Quarry. The right of way has been diverted and instead of going straight across to Wardlow, you turn left and guided by large acorn signs walk 1/2 mile around the lefthand side of the quarry to a stile. Here turn left to another and walk along the field edge to a gate. Cross the B6417 road to a stile and cross the next field along its lefthand edge at first, to a stile and the A52 road. Turn left passing the Staffordshire and Peak Arts Centre at Caldonlow to the road junction at Hoften's Cross opposite the Cross Inn. Turn right and descend the road soon coming to your earlier route from Waterhouses and retrace your steps past the Yew Tree Inn and through the village of Cauldon back to the car park.

LONGER ROUTE FROM RAMSHORN - Turn right along the road to Wootton 1 1/2 miles away. En route pass the entrance to Kevin Quarry before getting superlative views of the Weaver Hills. At the road junction in Wootton keep straight ahead and turn left down Back Lane. In 60 yards before a house on your left on the righthand bend turn left to a stile. Ascend to the left of the house and continue ascending the fields guided by stiles to the righthand end of the Weaver Hills. Gaining the minor road - Back Lane - via a stile. Turn right then left through a gate and keep the limestone wall on your immediate right as you descend and ascend. On the otherside gain Wetside Lane a splendid track which you descend to a gate and lane. Turn left and cross the A52 road and walk past Dale Abbey Farm.

1/2 mile later pass Stanton Dale Farm on your left and the impressive limestone hill of Dale Tor. Just after turn left onto a walled track - Dale Lane - and follow this track for almost a mile to its junction with one from Huddale. Continue ahead keeping to the dale floor and in 1/2 mile reach a junction. Leave the track here at the stile and continue straight across the field and across the track from Middlehills Farm. Descend to the road to the right of the buildings and towers of Caldonlow Quarry. Here is a wooden stile. Turn right and in a few yards turn right into the Waterhouses car park.

OBSTRUCTION OF RIGHT OF WAY

Description of Right of Way
(e,g, "Footpath from Dovedale to Ilam")

_____
_____
_____

Nature of Obstruction
(e.g. Locked gate, barbed wire across path etc.,)

_____
_____

Location of Obstruction
(Give Grid Reference if possible.)

_____
_____

Date of discovery of obstruction

_____

Name and address of person making report -

_____
_____
_____
_____

- you may photocopy this form -

Send to -

the local Rambler's Association
Footpath officer
or
The Footpath Inspector,
Staffordshire County Council

CONSALL AND CAVERSWALL - 18 MILES

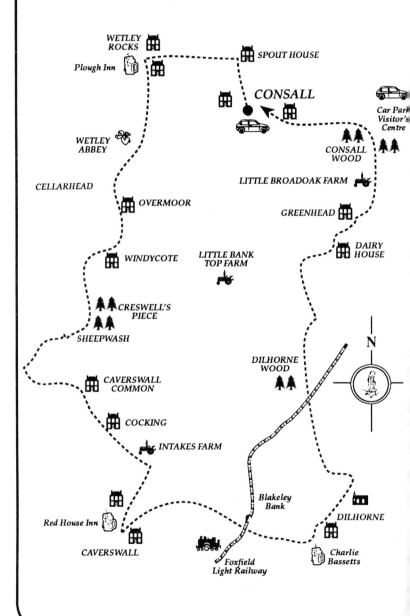

WETLEY ROCKS

Plough Inn

SPOUT HOUSE

CONSALL

Car Park Visitor's Centre

WETLEY ABBEY

CONSALL WOOD

CELLARHEAD

LITTLE BROADOAK FARM

OVERMOOR

GREENHEAD

WINDYCOTE

LITTLE BANK TOP FARM

DAIRY HOUSE

CRESWELL'S PIECE

SHEEPWASH

N

CAVERSWALL COMMON

DILHORNE WOOD

COCKING

INTAKES FARM

Blakeley Bank

DILHORNE

Red House Inn

Charlie Bassetts

CAVERSWALL

Foxfield Light Railway

CONSALL AND CAVERSWALL
- 18 MILES
- allow 7 hours

- Consall - Spout House - Wetley Rocks - Wetley Abbey - Overmoor - Cresswell's Piece - Sheepwash - Caverswall Common - Caverswall - Dilhorne - Dilhorne Wood - Dairy House - Greenhead - Consall Wood - Consall.

O.S. MAP - 1:25,000 Pathfinder Series Sheet No. 809 (SJ 84/94) - Stoke on Trent.

P - No official one in Consall village. Car park at Consall Nature Park 1 1/2 miles from route - this can be used to extend the walk to 20 miles!

- Plough Inn, Wetley Rocks; Red House Inn, Caverswall; Charlie Bassetts, Dilhorne.

ABOUT THE WALK - A walk around the south-western side of the Staffordshire Moorlands area. I really enjoyed this walk exploring a totally new area passing through rolling countryside and woodland to unspoilt villages full of character and hidden gems. Much of the route is on little used rights of way and you will have to be alert to find some of the stiles - they are all there - except in three places. But I hope this walk will encourage you to explore this fascinating and scenic area and safeguard some of the lesser known paths. It is worth exploring Caverswall to see the church, castle and stocks - the inn is a welcome halt and the halfway point! Dilhorne is exceptional with an impressive gatehouse of a former hall. The church has the only octagonal tower in Staffordshire. I have started the walk from the centre of Consall village but you can start from the car park at Consall Nature Park, adding 2 miles to the walk.

WALKING INSTRUCTIONS - Starting from the T junction in the centre of Consall village walk eastwards along the road towards the Consall Nature Park for a few yards to footpath sign - "Folly Lane - 1 miles" and track on your left. Turn left down this to a stile and continue ahead on a grass track to the gate infront of Knowlbank. Go slightly right between the buildings to a stile on the otherside and continue along the righthandside of the fields to Spout House farm. Walk around it to your left to the farm track and walk past the farmhouse on your right. Continue on the track to your left to Folly Lane. Cross the lane to a stile and path sign and keep the field boundary on your left to reach the stiles. After the third stile you walk along a walled path to the drive of Long Meadows Farm, which you descend to the A522 road at Wetley Rocks.

Cross over to your right and descend Plough Bank to the Plough Inn at the bottom. Turn left and left again into Randles Lane, footpath signed - "Cellarhead". At first it is a tarmaced surface as you pass the playing fields on your right but soon becomes a track and after Abbey Grange Farm, a path. Keep straight ahead on the defined path and past a small pond on your left as you pass Wetley Abbey well on your right. Keep straight ahead on a track past the outbuildings on your immediate right. At the end of the buildings is a stile and bear right across the field to another stile. Descend to a wide footbridge and stile and a few yards later another stile. Here turn left and keep the hedge on your right to the track at Gate House. Beyond the house bear left and around the field edge on your left to reach a stile in the hedge, path sign and the A52 road at Overmoor - approx 888 ft. a.s.l. - Cellarhead is to your right.

Turn left and in a few yards turn right along March Lane. Opposite the first house in 20 yards, turn right through the gate and follow the track along the lefthand side of the field to a small farm. Go through the gate and right through the farmyard to another gate. Continue to a beech tree and along the field edge keeping the fence on your left. At the top of the field there is no stile but a gate to your right. Go through this and turn right along the track to Windycote. Walk through the farmyard and round to your right to a gate on your left. Turn left along the fenced grass track and begin descending to another gate and to a stile on your left. Go through this and continue descending with the field edge on your right and reach a track. Follow this to your left and in a few yards where it turns sharp right leave it on the corner by the black stile.

Keep straight ahead to another black stile before turning slightly left to another on the edge of Creswell's Piece wood. The pathline is not well defined at first but is a grassy sward through the trees for 200 yards. You can see perimeter of the wood on your right and angle down to the left of it and cross a small stream. Continue ahead angling upwards and the pathline soon becomes a distinct track as you meander through the woodland for nearly 1/2 mile to the track close to Sheepwash. Follow this track round to your right for 1/2 mile to the Leek road - A520. Just before it turn left onto another track and in 1/4 mile follow this round to your right. Keep straight ahead into a minor road passing a rugby field on your right before reaching a crossroads at Roughcote.

Turn left along the road to Caverswall Common. In a 1/3 mile close to the summit of the area - 771 ft - turn right infront of Higherland Farm and follow the track. Keep straight ahead on this track as it descends and ascends past Cocking. Continue ahead and ignore the fork to your left and where it turns sharp right to Intake Farm go over the stile and walk along the field edge to another stile and minor road from Caverswall. Turn right and in a 1/3 mile along the lane the road curves left. At the far end of the bend is a stile on your right. Cross the field diagonally to your left to a gate and descend to another infront of a house. Turn right then left along a track to the minor road - The Hollow - from Caverswall. You can turn left here to continue the walk but it is worth seeing Caverswall a few yards away to your right - there are the stocks to see, the Red House Inn, and church and nearby castle.

Return to The Hollow and ascend the lane to just past your earlier path to a path on your right leading to a stile. Continue in the field beyond keeping to the righthand side to reach another stile and another before a track. Cross over to a stile and walk along the lefthand edge of the field passing Tunstall Sytch on your left to a stile. Bear right to reach two more stiles. Ascend the field to the hedge but there is no stile here. Descend the other side to your right to a stile before a road. Cross over to a stile and reach the Foxfield Light Railway. Cross the tracks to a stile and ascend the field to the top righthand corner where there is a stile. On you left is Blakeleybank. Descend the field towards the bottom lefthand corner where there is a stile. Cross the next field corner to another and basically keep parallel with the road on your right to reach a further stile and emerge onto the road on the immediate lefthand side of Charlie Bassetts Inn. Turn left along New Road into Dilhorne passing All Saints church on your right and as you descend the otherside of the small hill the entrance gate to former Dilhorne Hall, whose grounds are know a recreational area.

Shortly afterwards turn left, as footpath signed, and descend a track down to a fishing pond. Follow the track around it and before the small car park turn right to a stile. For little over the next 1/2 mile you basically keep straight ahead. At first it is a grass track that curves right then left. Keep to the right of a small wood and you will see and reach all the stiles - five of them - to gain the Foxfield Light Railway.

Cross over to a stile and walk beside the fence on your left into Dilhorne Wood. In 200 yards bear right still keeping the fence on your left to the woods perimeter and a stile. Turn left at the stile and ascend the field keeping to the righthand side. At the top follow the wall around to your right to a gate. Follow the track beyond to your right to a minor road in 1/4 mile. Turn left along it and in just over 1/4 mile where it turns left is a wooden stile. Ascend this and turn right - there is no stile here. Descend the field with the fence on your right to a gate. Continue ahead but there is no stile at the end of the field. Continue descending and reach a splendid pair of stiles with stone steps! Descend the next field to a stile and at the end of the next reach a gate. Turn right and follow the track towards Dairy House.

Just before the buildings turn left at the stile and pathsign. Cross the field keeping to the righthand side to a stile. Continue ahead to another stile by a solitary tree. Aim for the lefthandside of Greenhead Farm and reach the stiles and road at Greenhead. Turn left then right along the narrow lane to Broadoak. Approaching the houses, little over 1/4 mile later pass over a stile and walk between the two farms, descending the field close to its boundary on your right. The path is discernable and marked with white painted posts. Where it steepens follow the signed path round to your right and descend to a stile and into Consall Wood. Cross the stream and ascend to the main path in the wood - if you turn right here you will reach the car park and visitors centre at Consall Nature Park. Cross the path and ascend on a defined path to the top corner of the wood. Continue ahead just inside the wood with its boundary on your left to a fence - no stile here. Continue along the field to a stile on your left. Go through this and keep the field edge on your right and after three fields reach the track from Upper Farm. Follow this through the farmyard to the road in Consall village, beside the path sign - "Hollins 1 1/4 miles". To your right is where you began several hours ago!

WALK RECORD CHART

Date walked

THE RIVER DANE - 13 MILES ....

LONGNOR & WARSLOW - 12 MILES ....

THE ROACHES - 16 MILES...

ROUND TITTESWORTH RESERVOIR - 8 MILES ....

TITTESWORTH & RUDYARD RESERVOIRS

- 14 MILES ....

BIDDULPH MOOR - 12 MILES ....

CALDON CANAL & KNYPERSLEY RESERVOIR

- 20 MILES ....

ONECOTE & COOMBES VALLEY - 18 MILES ....

BUTTERTON AND RIVER HAMPS - 12 MILES ....

ALSTONEFIELD - 12 MILES ....

FOUR STAFFORDSHIRE VILLAGES - 8 MILES ....

ILAM ROCK - 8 MILES ....

THE CHURNET VALLEY & WEAVER HILLS

- 13 & 15 MILES ....

CONSALL AND CAVERSWALL - 18 MILES ....

GET A JOHN MERRILL LONG WALK BADGE - Complete six of these walks and send a copy of the Walk Record Chart and £2.50 to J.N.M. Publications for a signed certificate and badge - 3 1/2 diameter and four colour embroidered on a blue cloth.

BADGE ORDER FORM

Dates completed ....

....

Name

....

Address

....

....

"I've done a John Merrill Walk" T shirt - Emerald Green with white lettering - all sizes - £7.00 including postage and VAT.

From - J.N.M. Publications, Winster, Matlock,
                Derbyshire. DE4 2DQ

TEL. Winster - 0629 - 650454 (24 hrs.)
Fax: Winster - 0629 - 650 416

.... You may photocopy this form if needed ....